Itchy Feet
Travel Tales

in Asia

BOOKS 1 THROUGH 5

Also available as ebooks:

BOOK 1 Interrupting Cow: *Dropped Call • It all Comes Out in the Wash • Some Like It Hot • Local Wildlife: Monkey Business • Local Wildlife: Holy Cow • Welcome to China • Lost in Translation • From Breast ilk to Beer: Mongolian Drinking Stories • Trains, Pains, and Accidental Sightings*

BOOK 2 Bambi Ate My Yen: *Doctor's Orders • Tomato, Tomahto • Locker Room Talk • Lost in Translation: Korea • Haiku Hate • Karaoke in Japan • Local Wildlife: VeniZEN • Zeros Matter • Grandma's Kimchi Recipe • #TeachingInKorea • Just the Way You Are • SPAM Donor*

BOOK 3 No Standing on Toilet: *Et Tu, Taxi Traitor?! • Gaspers, Grumblers, Snufflers and Snorters • HOSTEL • Still Lost in Translation • Local Wildlife: Who Let the Dogs Out • Spirited Away • The Rooster and the Egg • Everybody Poops • Pics or It Didn't Happen*

BOOK 4 Chew Tentacle Thoroughly: *In an Octopus's Garden • Chopsticks: Whatever Wok's • Those Who Don't Shout Don't Eat • Ruined Restaurants and Hidden Gems • Easy on the Soy Sauce, Old Man • A Whiter Shade of Pale • #TeachinginNam • Mr. Mufflerplucker • Slaughter in the School Zone • Racial Slurs in Context • Holiday in Cambodia • A Wet Man Never Fears the Rain*

BOOK 5 You Like a Pho?: *No, the Other Pho • Pipe Dreams • Betel Mania • I Love the Smell of Silkworm in the Morning • At the Movies • Scamburgers in Scambodia • Happy Pizza • Walkabout*

Itchy Feet
Travel Tales
in
Asia

BOOKS 1 THROUGH 5

SAM LETCHWORTH

www.fermatahouse.com

ITCHY FEET TRAVEL TALES IN ASIA — 5 BOOKS IN 1: Interrupting Cow, Bambi Ate My Yen, No Standing on Toilet, Chew Tentacle Thoroughly, and You Like a Pho? is an omnibus of Books One through Five in the series, Itchy Feet Travel Tales in Asia. Copyright © 2020 by Sam Letchworth. Manufactured in the United States of America. All rights reserved. No part of this publication may be reproduced, stored in a retrieval system, or transmitted, in any form or by any means—electronic, mechanical, photocopying, recording, or otherwise—without prior written permission, except for brief quotations in critical reviews or articles.

ISBN 978-1-947566-11-8

Library of Congress Control Number: 2021915464

Published by Fermata House: Versailles, Kentucky
www.fermatahouse.com

Cover design by 16Acres

Cover and chapter title fonts:
 Ink Free by Steve Matteson
 Janitor by JLH Fonts
 Opera-Lyrics by Dennis Bathory-Kitsz

Disclaimer:
The voices of the beloved characters in this book are recorded dutifully and with the utmost affection.

Particularly the Australians.

Photos:
View the photos in this book in their original size, resolution, and color at:
www.fermatahouse.com/itchyfeet/photos.

Review:
You can help make the Itchy Feet Travel series more accessible to others by leaving a review on amazon.com.

Amazon's search engine has an algorithm for visibility which is largely based on the number of reviews a book receives. Just a few words will suffice. Thanks!

To everyone
who gave me meat when I hungered,
who gave me drink when I was thirsty,
who took this stranger in...

you know who you are.

To stay updated on new Itchy Feet Travel Tales, visit:
www.itchyfeetbooks.com
www.fermatahouse.com/itchyfeet

CONTENTS

BOOK ONE ~ INTERRUPTING COW

Intro	Burmese Leeches and Waterlogged Words	11
1	Dropped Call	15
2	It All Comes Out in the Wash	19
3	Some Like It Hot	21
4	Local Wildlife: Monkey Business	28
5	Local Wildlife: Holy Cow!	31
6	Welcome to China	35
7	Lost in Translation	38
8	From Breast Milk to Beer — Mongolian Drinking Stories	40
9	Trains, Pains, and Accidental Sightings	46

BOOK TWO ~ BAMBI ATE MY YEN

10	Doctor's Orders	52
11	Tomato, Tomahto	58

12	Locker Room Talk	61
13	Lost in Translation: Korea	64
14	Haiku Hate	67
15	Karaoke in Japan	71
16	Local Wildlife: VeniZEN	73
17	Zeros Matter	75
18	Grandma's Kimchi Recipe	80
19	#TeachingInKorea	84
20	Just the Way You Are	91
21	SPAM Donor	93

BOOK THREE ~ NO STANDING ON TOILET

22	Et Tu, Taxi Traitor?!	98
23	Gaspers, Grumblers, Snufflers and Snorters	105
24	HOSTEL	110
25	Still Lost in Translation	115
26	Local Wildlife: Who Let the Dogs Out	118
27	Spirited Away	120
28	The Rooster and the Egg	124
29	Everybody Poops	133
30	Pics or It Didn't Happen	137

BOOK FOUR ~ CHEW TENTACLE THOROUGHLY

| 31 | In an Octopus's Garden | 144 |

32	Chopsticks: Whatever Wok's	149
33	Those Who Don't Shout Don't Eat	152
34	Ruined Restaurants and Hidden Gems	155
35	Easy on the Soy Sauce, Old Man	158
36	A Whiter Shade of Pale	161
37	#TeachingInNam	164
38	Mr. Mufflerpluckcr	172
39	Slaughter in the School Zone	175
40	Racial Slurs in Context	178
41	Holiday in Cambodia	181
42	A Wet Man Never Fears the Rain	185

BOOK FIVE ~ YOU LIKE A PHO?

43	No, the *Other* Pho	188
44	Pipe Dreams	193
45	Betel Mania	196
46	I Love the Smell of Silkworm in the Morning	202
47	At the Movies	205
48	Scamburgers in Scambodia	210
49	Happy Pizza	213
50	Walkabout	222
	Photo Acknowledgements	232

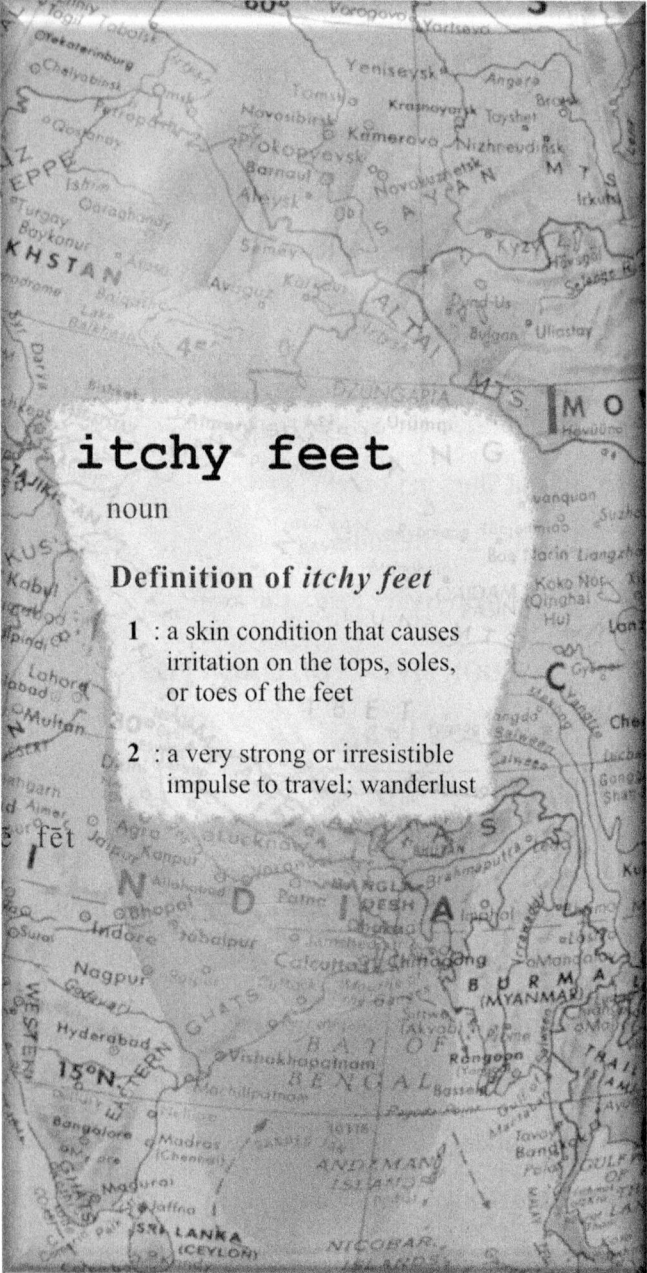

itchy feet
noun

Definition of *itchy feet*

1 : a skin condition that causes irritation on the tops, soles, or toes of the feet

2 : a very strong or irresistible impulse to travel; wanderlust

Intro

Burmese Leeches and Waterlogged Words
ဒါကဖြစ်ရပ်မှန်ပါ

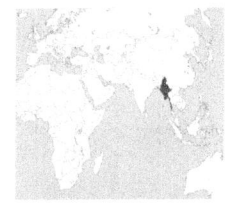

I picked the leeches off my river-soaked skin. Stripped down to my birthday suit. There was another leech on the inside of my inner thigh.

I pulled the slippery, squirming thing from its suctioned grasp and tossed it into the campfire. Blood was running down my legs, my arms, my torso in thin streaks.

"On the bright side," I said, breaking the silence, "I got to burn some of these little bloodsucking bastards at the stake."

Tan laughed. "Fried leech-ee. Hope you are hungry."

Tan was our guide on this trek through the backyard of Myanmar's Shan State. This traditional longyi-skirt-wearing, betel-nut-chewing, pepper-picking beauty of a man had just saved my life.

I turned my attention to my drenched backpack that had been submerged in the raging river current right along with me. I dug for my leather-bound travel diary. It was soaked through. Ruined. All of those stories, from all of my travels. Ruined. Pages and pages pasted together. The ink already bleeding out.

I folded up, naked, on the grass, and put my head between my knees.

Tan came over to comfort me. He put his hands on my shoulders and whispered, "It will be ok."

For the next hour, Tan sat on his haunches in front of the fire and held my leather-bound diary over the flames, methodically peeling page from page and drying them out, one by one.

Without Tan, this book would be incomplete, or nonexistent. What's more, without Tan (and the steady

hand of "Dimitri The Barefoot"), I might very probably be dead.

The following stories, lifted as they were recorded in that very journal, are 99% true.

However, what with the water damage and all, the ink may have run.

Just a little bit...

```
Here's Tan, comparing the size of his
pepper with mine.

And don't worry, this isn't the last
you'll hear of Tan. Later you'll read
the story of how he led our group across
a raging river. (Chapter 50 "Walkabout")
```

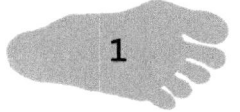

Dropped Call
မစင်အစာစားခြင်း

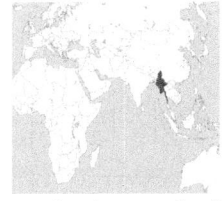

There's dropping your phone in a toilet, and then there's dropping your phone in a Myanmar squatter. They call it a squatter because that's the position you assume while perched over the hole in the ground.

It's all in the thighs.

This particular squatter was in an outhouse behind a bar in Shwenyaung, Myanmar. The rickety plywood door had loops for a lock, but no hook. I jammed a chopstick into the loops to keep the door closed while I went about my emergency quadricep workout.

When travelling through developing countries, you're going to be on your haunches — a lot — with no toilet paper for miles. In places like Myanmar and India, your "toilet paper" is a bucket of water placed conveniently to the left of the hole you're hovering over.

And, you guessed it — there's a reason why it's insulting to touch someone with your left hand, because it's been where the sun don't shine.

This standard squatter is palatial compared to the one in this story.

There I was, crouched over the worst toilet in Myanmar. Rats scurried about the corners of the privy. I played on my phone to distract from the reality of the situation.

Thanks to the *lephet thoke* I had for lunch, this one was a knuckle-biter, and my trembling thigh muscles were protesting the lengthy squatting session. As I attempted to reposition myself, the phone slipped from my hand and fell right into the abyss.

> **LEPHET THOKE**
>
> A salad of fermented tea leaves.
>
> Though this is the most popular Burmese dish, I would describe the smell as a wet dog's prolapsed anus.

I'd like to say I bid that phone adieu and never looked back. But, cheap bastard that I am, I rescued it from the depths of Hell and plunged it into the bucket of water beside me. Even the rats looked on in disgust.

I took my befouled phone back to the hostel, grabbing a bag of dry rice along the way. Once there, I took a bowl from the kitchen, poured in the rice, and buried my phone deep within it. (This is actually a great life-hack for drying out a wet phone, as the rice absorbs the moisture and usually returns the phone to working condition.)

I left it there for about 12 hours. I pulled out my Samsung the next morning and, voila! She was alive again, no worse for the wear. I went about my day of strolling around the town and even treated myself to an oil foot massage.

When I returned to the hostel that evening, I noticed that the bowl of rice, which had absorbed the particle waste of a hundred Burmese men, was gone.

Guests were convening in the common room around the table.

The little Burmese lady that ran the hostel emerged from the kitchen and greeted me. "Will you join us for family meal tonight?"

"Absolutely," I replied. It's always a treat when anyone, anywhere, prepares a home-cooked meal. "What's for dinner, mama?"

"It is favorite here in Shan State. We call it *nga htamin*. You are ok with fish?"

"Sounds amazing. I haven't eaten all day," I smiled, and sat down at the table.

Out came the food. Nga htamin, it turns out, is a dish made with turmeric, fish flakes and garlic oil that's been squashed into rice. Also known as "Shan-style Rice."

Our house mama made her way around the table, scooping out generous servings.

She picked up my plate.

"Mama? Where did you get this rice?"

"Someone leave big bowl on the balcony. You know my house rule — any food leave out belong to the house."

I stared at the baseball-shaped rice clump in front of me.

"You know what?" I said, excusing myself. "I forgot. I have to make a phone call."

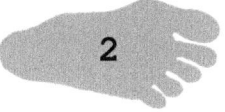

It All Comes Out in the Wash
ซักชุดชั้นในเหม็น ๆ

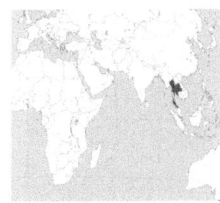

Paying $1 per kilo to have dirty clothes locally laundered in Chiang Mai, Thailand sure beats washing your week's worth of sweaty socks in the sink.

But don't forget to say a prayer to the Laundry Gods.

With at least two dozen loads of as many people's coloreds and whites going at any given hour down at the Changklan Road laundromat, things are going to get mixed up. The batch you brought in won't always be the batch you take home.

If the Laundry Gods have smiled on you that day, you'll end up with new and exciting articles of clothing. If the Laundry Gods are displeased with you, well, there goes your favorite Metallica t-shirt. It's just the way the powdered detergent crumbles.

And that's how I ended up with this pair of sweet, calf-length socks with embroidered Viking hats. If by chance the owner of these socks is out there reading this now, I'm sorry, but you're never getting them back.

Of course, that means that you are in possession of my boxer shorts. (They're the cotton ones with little gnomes on them.)

And the great karmic spin-cycle keeps on tumblin' around.

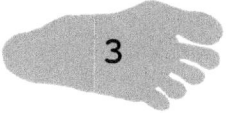

Some Like It Hot
매워주세요

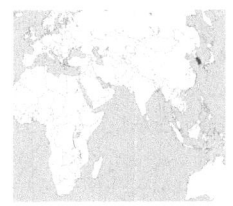

I didn't know I liked Korean food. Hell, I didn't even know what Korean food was until I moved there and learned how to read the Korean Hangeul character script off of a short-order menu. From that point on, it was a love affair.

Open 24/7, Kimbab Cheonguk, or "Kimbab Heaven," is the Denny's of Korea. *Kimbab* is the Korean version of a sushi roll. Not quite a meal, it's commonly eaten as a snack on the go.

The *Heaven* part is what's worth focusing on — the ladies at Kimbab Cheonguk will make you any Korean dish you could desire, so long as you know how to order it.

I knew if I ordered a traditionally spicy dish like kimchi-jiggae or maeundae galbijjim, those aunties at the local kimbab shop would see my pasty white ass and water it down. I needed to ensure that they did no such thing. So, when I moved to Seoul to teach English, the first phrase I learned in Korean was *Doh mebgay hey joo-say-oh*. (Make it spicy, please.)

Some like it hot.

Personally, I like my Korean soup at about 10,000 units on the Scoville Scale. Wilbur L. Scoville developed the Scoville Organoleptic Test in 1912. The Scoville Scale measures the hotness of a chili pepper and/or its sauce.

> It's a little known fact that Wilbur's own wife rated him a solid 8,048 on the Scoville Scale. This kept Wilbur up at nights until Mrs. Scoville reassured him that she had never been with anyone who scored 8,049 or higher. Little did Mrs. Scoville know that Wilbur had rated her lower. Much lower.

I could tell that the aunties at Kimbab Heaven had been gradually increasing the Scoville hotness level with each soup they served me. But it was still never quite hot enough. This was wintertime, and I needed a proper sinus exorcism.

I walked in from the cold. "Jeogiyo!" I cried out, taking off my gloves and finding my favorite window booth.

"Neeeeeh!" came the response from the kitchen ladies.

ITCHY FEET TRAVEL TALES 23

"Marco!" I shouted. "Polo!" they shouted back. Yeah, I came here a lot. It's safe to say these aunties, or *adjumas*, knew me.

My adjuma, Mi-Sook, came around. "An yeong, Sam-Sam," she smiled. "Sam" is the Korean title for teacher. It's used after your first name: Keith-Sam, Rachel-Sam, Leonardo-Sam.

I am Sam-Sam. Sam-Sam I am.

"Hanna may-oon jjampong, moon-eo bay," I told her, taking off my coat. (One dish of spicy seafood soup, no octopus.) After my traumatizing experience eating live octopus on New Year's, I made a point of always saying "NO Octopus!" when I ordered food in Korea.

> Read the harrowing tale:
> "In an Octopus's Garden" in Chapter 31.

But this time when I ordered it extra spicy, I threw in a curse word for effect. "Doh mebgay hey joo-say-oh, *JEBAL!*"

Mi-Sook raised her eyebrows. I nodded and winked. She smirked, shook her head, and went back to the kitchen. I heard an uncharacteristic commotion of laughter. The aunties at Kimbab Heaven were plotting to test my true picante potential.

While Korean food may have a reputation for heat, they can't really produce the hottest of hot peppers that you might expect from Thai or Mexican cuisine. The Korean peninsula is too far north of the equator. The hotter the climate, the hotter the pepper. Makes sense.

So what the Koreans do is employ a pepper extract called capsaicin. This is the crack of hot sauces, with all the potency of a pepper reduced down to a droplet. Just a dab will do ya. Yeah, it's cheating. But if you want to "go hot or go home," it's what's for dinner.

Dear Auntie Mi-Sook brought out my bubbling soup in a typical *deol sot* stone bowl. In tow behind her was the entire kitchen staff. She set the boiling red business in front of me and sat down with all the other adjumas at the table directly across from me. Each woman had her elbow on the table, her chin perched on her fist, watching me between snickers and shushings. The witch's coven was in session for this seance, and there was black majik in my bowl.

I stared into my jjampeong. Thick, Udon noodles rose to the surface with whole clams in the shell, scaly fishy bits, and little shrimps, all seething in a sea of vermillion heat.

I stirred it around with my metal chopsticks, took a deep whiff, and sneezed violently. One of the adjumas shricked. No one blessed me or wished me good health.

They don't really do that in Korea. When you sneeze, you're on your own.

I had made a tall pile of napkins for just such eventualities. Gazing back into my cauldron of hellfire, a piece of octopus tentacle floated to the surface. I deftly plucked it out of the soup with my chopsticks. "No octopus!" I said, and held it out to Mi-Sook, hot sauce dripping onto the table.

"Aniyo, aniyo!" she screamed, shaking her head vigorously and waving her hands. I dropped the foul thing onto a napkin.

I started with the rice pasta. I slurped up that first big nightcrawler noodle until it went smack and splattered my face with red. It took about three seconds for the capsaicin to catch up. My tongue went numb, my brow broke out in sweat, and the devil himself wrapped his reptilian fingers around my throat and squeezed. I choked, coughing harshly and wiping my forehead. The adjummas fell apart with laughter.

It was on now. I had asked for it, and boy had they given it to me. I figured speed was the best strategy. I sucked, swilled, guzzled and gulped, blowing my nose between bites into napkin after napkin until my nose was raw and I was barricaded by a wall of little clumped-up tissues.

From the peanut gallery, laughter had turned to ooh's and ahh's. Now the entire restaurant was in on it. Families and couples having their evening supper of mild bibimbap and kimchi soup were getting a show with their dinner. "Step right up and watch the white man eat the hottest shit ever, until steam comes whistling out of his ears." I'm here all week, folks.

"Mebgay?" asked Mi-Sook.

"Spicy?!" I grunted. "It's not spicy. It's perfect, damn you."

I picked up the stone bowl, brought it to my lips, and drank the remaining fiery juice. There was a rogue clam shell at the bottom. I clenched it between my teeth, sucked sharply, and spat it back into the bowl with an audible "ding!" I wiped my mouth with my shirt sleeve and emitted a primal, guttural belch.

The entire dining room erupted in applause. I stood up and took a bow. I put on my coat and my gloves, pulled out a fiver Korean Won note, and threw it down on the table.

"Cum som ni dah," I proclaimed, and walked out the door, the adjummas jumping up to slap me on the back.

I ran immediately to the corner store and grabbed a bottle of milk from the cooler. I tossed off the cap and chugged like a newborn to the teat. It tasted like honey butter. Koreans are always adding honey butter to perfectly good things. (Honey butter Cheetos, honey butter beef jerky, honey butter cigarettes.)

I couldn't care less in the moment, as I bathed in the stuff that ran down my chin, onto my coat, onto the floor.

I was laid up in bed for three days. When I had recovered enough to have an appetite again, I went back to my Kimbab Heaven. Mi-Sook shuffled to greet me.

"Doh mebgay hey joo-say-oh?" she said with a smirk.

"You know what, Mi-Sook?" I said. "I think I'm going to retire that phrase. Gimme some nice, bland dumplings."

```
This was my personal bottle of capsaicin
sauce. Approximately 500,000 on the
Scoville Scale.

In a year, I made it to about this little
fellow's hat.

I had to leave it behind.

Sad.

It would have been a lifetime supply.
```

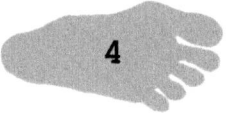

Local Wildlife: Monkey Business
Monyet Gila

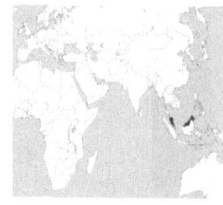

From the Indian subcontinent all the way to the South China Sea, the red-faced, red-assed rhesus macaque monkey is everywhere you want to be.

They are sneak-thieves, harassing and mugging the local populace. They steal lunches and phones. They break windows and destroy power lines. They have even been reported to kidnap babies from their cribs. The Hindus have further encouraged these fiendish imps by deifying a half-monkey god named Hanuman. But these macaques are roving gangs of terrorists, and they must be stopped.

Of course, I wasn't yet aware of their infamy when I visited the Batu Caves just outside Kuala Lampur, Malaysia.

The Batu Caves are a collection of Hindu temples built right into the caverns that rest high on a limestone hill. It's 272 steps straight up. And all along those steps, there are hundreds of these little guys. They are ever lurking. Watching from behind their menacing little demon eyes. Yawning and screeching and baring their fangs.

Monkeys scampered and darted across my path throughout my cardio climb to the top. After taking in

the magnificent Hindu shrines, I was ready to head back down. I had a bag of banana chips and thought, hey, what a great photo op. I'll feed the monkeys one by one, doling out banana bits into their little hands.

Idiot.

The very moment I produced the bag, the mob came swarming. A large male swooped in and snatched the bag right out of my hand. Some of his buddies followed him to fight over it. Others decided I must have more where that came from. I felt little grabbing hands all over me, pulling at my shirt, my trousers, and my unmentionables. I sprinted down the stairs to get away. They gave chase. One jumped on my back. Another shrieked through his fangs and clawed my legs in frustration.

"Take your stinking paws off me, you damned dirty apes!" I shouted, spinning in circles and swatting at the foul creatures.

There was an Indian woman with two small children ascending the stairs in front of me. Upon seeing my moment of hysterical moronity, she shielded her kids behind her. They were crying.

She shook her head at me in wild-eyed disbelief. "You are so crazy!"

No, Lady. Just naive and stupid. Don't feed the animals. Especially when they are rhesus macaques.

Local Wildlife: Holy Cow!
हैमबर्गर्स चिल्लाते हुए

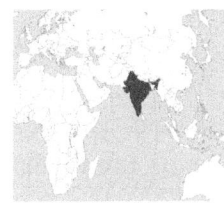

No, Hindus don't *worship* cows. They *revere* the cow as a sacred symbol of life. Makes sense — it's worth more alive than dead.

There's the milk, from which myriad cheeses and butters and ghee can be made.

Cow urine is used in Indian folk medicine to treat ailments from leprosy to cancer. It is also an effective floor cleaner.

And of course, cow crap makes the crops grow. I also hear that a peculiar mushroom grows out of it with some rather profound psychological effects. Maybe *that's* why they're so sacred...

Even McDonald's in India doesn't serve beef. Can you imagine? It's all chicken. The Hindus don't eat cows, the Muslims don't eat pigs, so they compromise on the chicken.

You know what they call a Big Mac in India? "The Chicken Maharaja Mac."

> *Two all-chicken patties, habanero sauce, lettuce, cheese, jalapenos, onions on a sesame seed bun!*

(I don't know what they call a Whopper, I didn't go to Burger King.)

The sacred cow thing can get out of hand sometimes. Every now and again you'll read a news story where a Muslim village in India has slaughtered a cow, and the nearby Hindu village catches wind of it, and they all grab machetes and run over to the Muslim village and slaughter everyone who slaughtered the cow. So I guess they take it pretty seriously.

Cows are everywhere in India. And I mean *everywhere.* Whole herds of them, owning the roads. They seem to be aware of their status, and they take full lazy advantage of it. No wonder the traffic is so bad.

I was drinking chai masala in a cafe in Varanasi when there was a banging and commotion at the back door. A cow burst its head through the wooden shutters with a loud "Muuuuhhhraaahhh!"

The little Indian lady at the counter threw up her hands and yelled at the cow in Hindi as she ran to fetch a bowl of corn. She fed it out of her hand while petting its head. When it was full, it snorted, backed itself out of the doorway, and ambled on down the street.

"That is the very special cow," she said, shaking bovine mucus off her hands. "There was a cow before her who would come visit like this every day at the same time. She died. She come back as this cow that you see. Now she come around and visit every day at the same time. She will not go until I feed her."

I was between sips of chai when Bessie barged in. She eyed me expectantly in the hopes that I would call her over to join me at my table.

Hindu cows are sacred, sure. But I did not know that this sanctity extended to their excrement.

With so many cows in India, there's that much more cow dung. Imagine — walking down the road, hopping and weaving and skipping over all the massive, stinking landmines.

But shit happens.

It happened to me in the Thar Desert.

I was in Jaisalmer, walking up the road to see that magnificent fortress way up on the hill, when I took my eyes off the road and went *splat*. Ankle-deep into a giant cow pie.

An Indian man in a white tunic was standing in front of his house. He clapped his hands in applause.

"Oh my friend, you are having such the good luck today!"

"I disagree," I replied, inspecting my crap-caked shoe.

"No!" he insisted. "To step in the fresh cow pattie is such the good luck! Lakshmi is shining down on you today, sir!"

"Do you think she'd find me lucky enough that there might be a water hose nearby?"

"Oh no." He beamed. "You must wear it proud, my friend!"

Lucky me.

Welcome to China
毛澤東的幽靈

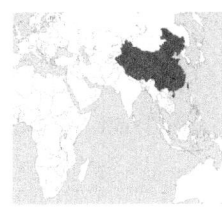

A tourist visa for entering China costs $140 US. That's egregious. Most Asian countries offer free entry to American citizens for at least one month. Even the Chinese-speaking countries of Taiwan, Hong Kong, and Macau (which China can't wait to gobble up and absorb into the People's Republic) are all free entry. Cambodia and Laos each want 30 bucks to come in. Myanmar charges a $50 visa fee —and those US bills had better be new and crisp.

Seeing as how I like to stretch my dollar out and keep the budget tight, I figured I'd just have to give China a miss.

That is, until I discovered a loophole in the system.

China allows you to visit without a visa IF you have a layover that is less than 72 hours. You just have to prove that you have an onward flight out of the country. This is known as the Transit Visa. Being that numerous Chinese cities are hubs for Asian air travel, this technicality is worth exploiting to get a taste of some authentic lo mein.

I was flying from Jakarta, Indonesia to Mongolia. This flight cost me $65, less than half the price of a Chinese tourist visa. I scheduled a layover in — you guessed it — China. A 72-hour layover, to be exact.

When I got off the plane in Beijing, I turned my phone back on while waiting in line at immigration. There was a cute Chinese girl behind me. She was being friendly or practicing her English or both.

"This is your first time in China?" she asked, smiling.

"Yes," I said. "Only for three days, I'm afraid."

"Welcome to China!" she beamed. "You are a traveler?"

"Yeah, sure." I said.

"Where do you travel?"

"So... I'm just coming from Indonesia. But before that, Taiwan, and before that —"

"Taiwan is China!" she interrupted.

"Right... Yeah, got it. I was in Hong Kong —"

"Hong Kong is China!" she sniped again, eyeing me sternly.

"Gotcha. Yep, Taiwan and Hong Kong are China. So, it's not my first time to China, I guess?"

I connected to the airport wifi on my phone. I tried to check all my top sites — Gmail, Facebook, Messenger. All blocked. I tried to watch a Youtube video while I stood in the immigration queue. No dice. When I tried to Google the reason why, I was also blocked.

"Hey," I turned back to her. "How come I can't access Google, Facebook, or Youtube?"

"Oh," she said, "you cannot. These websites are blocked. This is China."

"But I could access those sites in Hong Kong and Taiwan, even Macau —"

"This is China!"

Riiiiiight. Welcome to the People's Republic.

7

Lost in Translation
迷失在翻譯中

At least buy them dinner first.
SPOTTED IN JAPAN.

I hope the seafood gets the spaghetti home okay.
SPOTTED IN LAOS.

ITCHY FEET TRAVEL TALES 39

But it itches...
SPOTTED IN INDONESIA.

I'll have Number 47 please,
and hold the umbilical cord.
SPOTTED IN MYANMAR.

From Breast Milk to Beer — Mongolian Drinking Stories
Чингис хааны цээжинд

Mongolians are insane.

It's wonderful.

I was riding in a bus from Ulaanbatar, Mongolia to Kharkorum, the ancient capital. It was a four-hour journey across the barren landscape of the steppe. I was attempting to study the Cyrillic alphabet, when the rather large Mongolian woman in the seat next to me pulled up her shirt and let flop two juicy baby feeders with a *thud-thud*.

I fully support public breastfeeding — I just hadn't been that close to it since I myself was suckling at my mother's all those many years ago.

This woman was travelling with two children, a girl and a boy, aged about, oh, ten and twelve. I was looking around for the baby. Nope. Those two grown-ass children walked over from their seat across the aisle, scooped up one of mama's milk jugs apiece, shoved a big brown nipple in their mouths, and had a very loud snack.

The mother noticed me staring. Hell, I couldn't look away. She took one look at the expression on my face, threw back her head and cackled.

These ladies just keep the tit on tap in Mongolia.

The bus came to a screeching halt in the middle of the road, knocking the suckling kids onto the floor. I looked out the window — nothing but sky and desolate steppe. I was sure we had broken down in the middle of nowhere, when a young couple stood up and got off the bus. The engine roared back to life and we drove away as I watched them walk into the empty horizon.

> **Fun Fact:**
> China thought that the Gobi Desert was impassable until Genghis Khan crossed it with his Mongol Horde. The secret? They were all riding mares, which provided milk along the journey.

Historically, the Mongols only ate animal products. Meat and dairy. Not much has changed. The barbeque is worth writing home about. The dairy? Not so much.

They are still a largely nomadic people. Herdsmen move their yurts, (or, *ger*), each season out on the plains.

The official drink of Mongolia is *airag* — fermented horse milk. And yes, I have milked a horse. (Later they told me it was a male. I wondered why it only had one udder.)

Airag has about the same alcohol content as a beer, and people walk around town with 2-liter Coca Cola bottles filled to the brim with the foul, white stuff. I have even encountered airag that has been further distilled into vodka. (Don't forget to hold your nose when it's time for shots.)

> Mongolians are very, very proud of their shining moment in history when the Great Khans marauded the known world, chopping off all the heads as they went.
>
> They even named the bloody airport after it — I flew into Genghis Khan International from Beijing. Heck, the Mongols even founded the city of Beijing.
>
> (But don't remind China of that. It's a touchy subject.)

Here's an important travel tip: When in Mongolia, hide your beer.

I was traveling with my Canadian buddy, Mike. We planned on spending two weeks in Mongolia before catching the train straight up to central Siberia. From there we would ride the Trans-Siberian Railroad all the way west to Saint Petersburg over the next month.

Our timing had been perfect. We had unwittingly arrived in the Mongolian capital of Ulaanbatar on the opening day of the summer Naadam festival, or "The Three Games of Men." Established by Genghis Khan, the

games test three categories of skill: wrestling, archery, and horsemanship. The entire population of Mongolia had descended on the city for the occasion.

We had already booked, and paid for, our first night's stay in a hostel in the city center. But when we arrived that evening to check in, we discovered that the hostel had been over-booked. After a testy confrontation with the stern and stocky woman who ran the place, we made camp on the floor of a dark hallway upstairs.

Welcome to Mongolia.

The following morning, we promptly switched accommodation to another hostel nearby that actually had available beds, and then wandered bleary-eyed through the crowded streets to the festival grounds. Mike and I were enjoying some bottled beers on the street just outside the stadium where the wrestling was taking place.

A very stout, very drunk Mongolian man stumbled bow-legged towards us. Before I realized what was happening, he had snatched the beer out of my hand and chugged half of it, wiping his mouth with a satisfied grunt. He tried to hand it back to me.

"You know what?" I said. "You keep that one."

He grunted in approval, smiling wide and toothless, and shuffled off with my beer.

What a crazy guy, right? But this continued to happen everywhere we tried to enjoy a public frosty. Whenever a Mongolian man would zero in on us and begin lumbering over, eyeing the bottles in our hands, we would have to shotgun them as quickly as possible lest we surrender another beer to the thirsty hoard.

History tells us that the Mongol Conquests were basically the most epic pub crawl of all time. The Khans had a penchant for wine and indulged in every new variety that they discovered in each new conquered land. Many of the Khans died from alcoholism as a result.

So don't drink around the Mongols unless you've brought enough to share with the class.

Mike and me on Mongolian mares. They may look like ponies. But these are the same horses that won the Mongol Empire, bred for their hardiness and stamina.

9

Trains, Pains, and Accidental Sightings
ट्रेन स्टेशन की करी मत खाओ

My favorite way to travel is by train. The older and rustier, the better. I like the toss and rumble of a chooglin' locomotive. When the sound and vibration of popping gears on tracks gets in my bones, I feel one with the machinery. This is the most classic traveling experience for me, and it trumps the bus or the plane every time. Because, on a train across country, the journey *is* the adventure.

I have never slept better than being rocked to sleep on an Indian night train. That is, until it rolls into a stop and local hawkers board the passenger cars, parading up and down the aisles carrying tea kettles and food baskets and shouting, "Chai Masala! Samosa!" Toss a few coins into the hands of these peddlers before they hop back off the train, and you won't regret it. For this bleary-eyed traveler, a cuppa tea and a fried potato-and-onion pastry is a welcome treat to lull me right back to slumber. The steam whistle blows and the engine groans back to life and rumbles my metal womb.

India trains have different fare castes (er, classes). The high rollers sleep in the "AC" section. These air-conditioned cars have a choice of private cabins or open bunks with little privacy curtains. And, of course, they have better bathrooms.

The cheapest class is "General Seating." Passengers are herded like cattle, shoulder to shoulder in a sea of sweaty, raw humanity. On short journeys, I've boarded with the huddled masses, fighting over an open window for a breath of air. This is one step above riding on top of the train car itself. (Seriously. People actually do ride on top of the train.)

The most popular and most coveted tickets are in "Sleeper Class." No aircon or fresh linens here, and the toilets haven't been cleaned since India was British. But I always prefer this 3-bunk stacked carriage for its middle ground of authenticity and semi-comfort.

In Sleeper Class, there is always someone hanging out in your bunk when you board.

Sometimes they even move for you.

Once, on a train from Mumbai, traveling down the west coast to Goa, there were five young Indian men all sharing my reserved top bunk. I was too tired today for this.

"Namaste, dudes."

"Namaste." They all smiled back, and kept chatting amongst themselves in Hindi.

I tried the old passive-aggressive move — looking in confusion at my ticket, then up at the painted seat numbers, then back at my ticket. They finally got it. All five swung down off of my third-tiered bunk. I climbed up the metal rungs. I tossed off my backpack at the head of the mat and used it for a pillow. The train rolled out and I passed out.

I woke up at a stop and looked over at the top bunk across from mine. The five fellows had moved onto it, shoulder to shoulder, their knees together. They were all watching me intently. For how long, I don't know. I smiled awkwardly, and they beamed back, ear to ear.

"Namaste, dudes."

"Namaste," they all chimed in chorus, and continued to stare. I shook my head and rolled back over in the bunk.

When traveling in India, I associate almost exclusively with other men. There is a social sex segregation, with separate queues at banks and trains, even separate schools.

Outside of a more modern city like Mumbai, I rarely mingle with any Indian women except to conduct a business transaction or ask for directions. Which is a pity, because women from the subcontinent are vividly beautiful, with their brightly colored saree dresses, ornate belts, bejeweled headbands and delicate scarves.

I find them intimidating, but moreover I'm afraid to break any cultural taboos. (As I inadvertently did in Laos, where it is evidently illegal for a foreign man to be with a local woman.)

And I've certainly never approached a woman wearing a niqab.

Except this one time...

The niqab is often confused with the burqa as a blanket-term for all Islamic face veils. An actual burqa has a mesh screen for the woman to see out of. I honestly don't know how they walk around like that. The niqab, which is more common, has the unobscured, lateral eye-slit.

Ah, those eyes. The most radiant, piercing, soul-stealing eyes I have seen in my life have been the ones that peer out from behind the veil. I fall mysteriously in love every time.

The niqab is not an uncommon sight in India, where Islam is the second largest religion. On the street, I saw two women in full niqab ordering ice cream cones. How were they going to eat ice cream? I'd never thought about it before. I guess I had always assumed it was all one piece of fabric. It turns out it's a two-piece: the cowl and the veil. I watched in curious amazement as they lifted the veil with one hand and slid the cone underneath it, one lick at a time.

So, yeah. I've never approached a woman wearing a niqab.

Except this one time...

When I was on a train to Varanasi...

We were somewhere near the border of Uttar Pradesh when the food poisoning began to take hold.

The palak paneer curry I had eaten at the Old Delhi Railway Station just before boarding the train wasn't agreeing with me. The spinach puree was nice enough, but something was off about that homemade cheese. The paneer turned inside of me, curdling up in my gut.

Travelers affectionately call it the "Delhi Belly."

I proceeded to visit the train toilet every half-hour of our 13-hour journey en route from Delhi to Varanasi. It's bad enough squatting one out in a regular Indian hole-in-the-ground. But on a moving, bumping train, it's positively precarious. And with a bad case of the trot rot? That's just downright dangerous.

I assumed the position, bracing myself with both hands against the narrow walls as the train jostled down the track. The only view was straight down through the open hole in the floor. I watched my spinach curry spill out in the same color and consistency as it had gone in, splashing off the railroad ties that passed by below.

Seven hours in, I had already gone through my emergency TP. My new toilet paper was a bottle of water and my left hand. I was wiping with the locals now.

Back and forth I went from my bunk to the toilet in a weak-kneed walk of shame. I hadn't spoken to God in a while, and figured this was as good a time as any to start. I prayed each time I made that trip to please, Jesus, let this one be the last.

Were we on number nine now, Lord? I'd lost count. Doubled-over, I burst back into the bathroom.

She hadn't locked the door.

If I had ever been curious about what's going on under a niqab, I certainly wasn't curious any more.

It wasn't just a "lifting of the veil"—no, it's safe to say the whole curtain had gone up.

And, it appeared we had both eaten at the same curry place.

She looked up. Our eyes locked. I don't know whose were wider. A long, low gasp emitted from beneath her face covering and crescendoed into a high-pitched shriek.

I slammed the door shut. I hobbled at the best clip I could muster to the next train car toilet.

Had I unwittingly committed some grave sin? Did this mean I had to marry her now? I'd have to convert, of course. Fortunately, I had very recently opened up a new dialogue with God. I hovered on my haunches over the hell hole, and begged Allah's forgiveness.

For the rest of my time in India, whenever I passed a woman in a niqab, I always wondered if she was "the one…"

10

Doctor's Orders
넌 너무 세게 똥

Mr. Kim was a peculiar fellow. He was an austere Korean man who spoke English in a low, hushed voice, and would begin every sentence with a drawn-out, "Sooo…" Any time I talked to him, he would lean back and rub his belly with both hands, and sort of moan in "hmmmm's" and "haaaah's" wearing a wide grin. He overused the word "the" when he spoke English, especially when referring to people. "Sooo… The Sam," he would call me.

Mr. Kim was my boss.

As director of my English academy in Seoul, he roamed the halls during class time. He glided over the tile floors, skiing on the surface with his soft-soled shoes. When I passed him in the halls I always bowed low in customary Korean respect. He would nod back and ski on past me.

He was a good and decent man. He cut my paychecks on time and cared about my health. And, he always gave me a SPAM gift set on holidays. Yeah, that's a real thing in Korea. [See Chapter 21.]

He was also weirdly obsessed with making sure that we swept under the bed in our company-provided housing. He would close on this important point at the end of every staff meeting. "Sooo... make the sure to sweep under the bed. Is very important for the health."

Classes at the academy started at 4 p.m. Teachers were expected to be in the office, butt-on-chair at our cubicles by 2 o'clock sharp. Class prep took maybe an hour. And so it used to be that, around 3 o'clock, the teachers would all take an hour-lunch at one of the dozen Korean kitchens in the area.

Lunch was the highlight of our day.

But one dark day, a fellow foreign teacher broke protocol. He left the office almost as soon as he had arrived and took himself out for an entire kimchi and corn pizza. After he finished his pie, he went to a salon and got a haircut. Probably a mani-pedi too. His little rogue break had taken the entire two-hour planning period. He skidded into his first class just as the bell rang.

In response, Mr. Kim revoked our lunch hour. Eat the lunch before the school, he admonished us. And so we sat, from 2 to 4, keeping our desks warm, our stomachs growling with vexation towards our delinquent colleague.

After weeks of sitting in a chair for two hours every afternoon, I developed the ol' "seat squirms." When I couldn't sit still any longer, I knew it was time to make a doctor's appointment.

Going to the doctor with a translator is always fun. It's even more fun when that translator is your boss.

Mr. Kim had accompanied me to the doctor before for ailments such as the flu, a bronchial infection, and Athlete's Foot.

But *this* time I didn't need some ointment for foot fungus...

I'd been sitting uncomfortably in my office chair for an hour when Mr. Kim came to take me to the doctor. He was already donning a facemask, dangling one in his hand for me to wear. He always wore a mask on the street, so now we were twinsies, Mr. Kim and me. Long before Covid-19, Koreans were already wearing face masks to the point of fashion.

The clinic was one block around the corner. We had a muffled conversation from beneath our masks as we walked.

"Soo. You are the sick?"

"Well, not sick-sick, Mr. Kim. More of an... issue."

"Do you sweep under the bed?"

"Yes Mr. Kim, I sweep under the bed."

"Mmmm," he hummed in approval.

At the clinic, Mr. Kim spoke briefly to the nurse at reception, and we were ushered right into the doctor's office. No waiting around reading magazines and filling out paperwork. No weigh-in and blood pressure check. No bullshit.

The doctor's office was just that — an office. No sit-on-the-starchy-paper-of-the-examination-table while the doctor rolls around on a wheely chair business. Just a desk and two chairs. Mr. Kim and I sat down.

The doctor was an older gentleman with coke-bottle glasses and thick white hairs coming out of his ears. Mr. Kim launched into a fast-paced diatribe, to which the doctor nodded along. I had no idea what he possibly could have said.

"Sooo..." Mr. Kim turned to me. "What is the problem?"

The problem was a profound discomfort in my anus. Hemorrhoids, no doubt. How does one communicate *that*? I can't even spell hemmoroids. See? I just spelled it wrong. It isn't exactly the first vocabulary word you learn when taking up a second language.

I settled on, "I think I've got a grape on my asshole."

We all sat there for a moment. Nobody said anything. Mr. Kim and the doctor both stared at me, their brows furrowed.

"You know — cherry blossoms on my starfish. A candy-apple steamer. Low hanging fruit on the ol' balloon knot."

Still the same stare.

Mr. Kim broke the silence. His Korean to the doctor was much slower this time, as he searched for the right words.

The doctor nodded to Mr. Kim, then studied me with furrowed brow, then spoke to Mr. Kim.

Mr. Kim turned back to me. "Sooo... the doctor want to see that."

"Oh boy," I sighed. "Is that completely necessary?"

"Sooo... he is the doctor."

"Alright," I slapped my knees and stood up. "Let's do this then."

The doctor rose from his chair and waved me over. I walked around the desk and he motioned for me to bend over, pulling a pencil-sized flashlight from his lapel pocket.

I undid my belt and looked over at Mr. Kim. He was standing there watching, his hands folded on his belly and, I suspected, that repose of an odd grin beneath his mask.

"Mr. Kim. Do you mind, uh…"

"Oh," he said, "So sorry." He turned around to face the wall.

I slipped my trousers down to my ankles and bent over at a 90-degree angle. The doctor said something to Mr. Kim.

"Sooo… the doctor say to pull away the bottom."

"Thank you, Mr. Kim."

I grabbed my cheeks and spread 'em wide. I could see the doctor's feet upside down between my legs. With a grunt he got down on his haunches. I felt the heat of a flashlight all the way up into my small intestine.

"What's up there, Doc?" I asked, the blood rushing to my head. "Not a gerbil I hope."

"Ahh?" said the doctor.

"Nothing. Take your time in there, Doc."

The flashlight clicked off and the doctor pushed himself up off his thighs with another grunt. I popped up and pulled up my pants.

The doctor spoke to Mr. Kim, who was turned back around now.

"Sooo… the doctor say you have the *chi jil ha*." Mr. Kim hummed, searching for the English. "The grapefruit in the bottom hole."

"Grape," I corrected him, fastening my belt. "If there was a grapefruit down there we'd be in real trouble."

The doctor spoke again. Before Mr. Kim could give the translation, the doctor turned to me and, in English, said, "You are poop so hard."

"Uhh... okay?"

"Eat more kimchi," he said, again in English. I had to wonder if Korean doctors prescribe that to everyone, regardless of their symptoms.

"Would sitting in an office chair be a contributor to the *chi jil ha*?" I looked to Mr. Kim for a translation.

After some Korean back and forth, the reply came back, "Yes."

"So," I asked, "is more than one hour too long to sit in a chair?"

The translation came back again. Mr. Kim winced. "Sooo... the doctor say, not to sit in the chair for so long time."

The doctor wrote me a prescription for some topical cream and ordered me to stay off of the office chair.

And just like that, our lunch break was reinstated. I had taken one for the team. My coworkers owed me a big bowl of bibimbab for sure.

With extra kimchi.

Doctor's orders.

11

Tomato, Tomahto
화장실을 먹어

After two months in Korea, I'd had my fill of kimchi*. It was time to cleanse my palate with a good ole American garbage burger.

I followed my nose through the streets of East Seoul, sniffing out the familiar fart smell of processed beef and fry grease. My nose did not fail me. It led me directly to the Golden Arches. I flung open those double doors of nostalgia and jumped into the queue.

> ***Kimchi**
>
> This staple of the Korean diet is fermented cabbage made with red pepper sauce.
>
> See chapter 18: "Grandma's Kimchi Recipe."

The menu on the wall was in both English and Korean. My eyes scanned the more bizarre menu items, through shrimp burgers and seaweed fries, seeking out the "Quarter Pounder" — that "Royale with Cheese" (they got the metric system over there).

Apparently in Korea, it's known as simply, *Tomato Cheeseburger*.

I approached the counter with a Korean greeting of "An nyeong ha se yo," and a smile.

Then I confidently placed my order:

Hanna Tomato Cheeseburger, joosayoh.

(One Tomato Cheeseburger, please.)

The boy at the register replied with something unintelligible, but judging by the perplexed look on his face, obviously meant, "Say what now?"

Perhaps my American pronunciation of "to-*may*-toe" was confusing. I tried the British.

Hanna To-mah-toe Cheeseburger, joosayoh.

His response was the same.

Was my phrasing wrong? I'd practiced this one so hard! Then I flashbacked to the eighth grade class I had taught that afternoon. I was trying to break my students from the habit of adding, "UH," after just about every syllable they spoke in English. I imagined how young Dong Woo, one of the worst offenders, might pronounce my order.

I tried again, slowly.

Toe. Mahhh. Toe. Chee-juh Buh-guh-luh?

"Ah!" he said with a smile. "*Toe-Mah-Toe Chee-Juh-Buh-Guh-Luh!*"

And he handed me a tomato cheeseburger. It still, somehow, tasted like kimchi.

It's the little differences.

In Bangkok, Ronald McDonald welcomes me in honorific fashion. I love to explore the menu from country to country. In Germany, they've got bratwurst. In Thailand, they offer fried rice. I'm loving it.

12

Locker Room Talk
유에프시

The Korean language contains no sounds that are made with the teeth. No "F," "Th," or "V". Also, when speaking English, they insert vowels (like, "uh" and "ee") into words to better wrap their tongues around them. It's just the way their mouths are accustomed to moving.

This is known as Konglish — the incorporation and pronunciation of English words into the Korean language.

```
Can you translate this phrase from
Konglish back to English?

    Mah-yee
    pay-buh-lit-uh
    Ah-meh-lee-cahn
    hoe-lee-dae
    issuh
    Tank-uh-suh-gib-ing-uh.

Answer: My favorite American holiday is
Thanksgiving.
```

Six months into my tenure in Korea, I joined a gym to work off all the rice that had accumulated around my midsection. After a few weeks, I developed a rapport with MinJae, the desk guy, despite the fact that he didn't speak a word of English.

Korean gym locker rooms are social clubs where mostly older gentlemen stand around naked, chewing the fat whilst blow-drying their nether regions. Indeed, the Korean sauna, or *jimjilbang,* is a place to spend hours soaking in your birthday suit with other men. Very... Ancient Rome.

You can also spend the night in one of these places for cheap, albeit on a mat on the floor with about forty other people, but in a smart pair of provided starchy pajamas.

I had finished a workout at the gym, deftly navigating the locker room blow-dryer circle, and was out the door when MinJae waved me down.

"An nyeong ha se yo, buddy." I gave him a fist-bump.

"You a pussy?" he blurted. He flashed me two thumbs up and a wide grin.

"Come again?"

"You a pussy!" He lunged at me, spun me around, and attempted to put me in a chokehold. I threw his arms away and slid out of it.

I posted up with fists out. "What the hell, Minjae?!"

"Aniyo, Aniyo," he said, waving his hand. "No, no." He went to the desk and jotted something on a piece of paper and handed it to me.

"Ohhhh," I said, relaxing. "U.F.C."

"You a pussy!" he exclaimed again.

"Sure," I laughed. "I like U.F.C. Who doesn't enjoy watching two men fight to the death until the referee saves one of them at the last minute?"

"You a pussyeeee!" he cried, shadow boxing the air.

Later that week I went to Minjae's apartment. He provided *pajeon* pancakes and a refrigerator full of soju rice wine. We watched Connor McGregor of the "You-a-Pussy" beat the dog-crap out of somebody in the Octagon.

I assume Connor won, but I can't remember much past the third little green bottle.

13

Lost in Translation: Korea
번역에서 분실

Save the planet: Recycle your pets.
SEEN IN KOREA.

ITCHY FEET TRAVEL TALES 65

*If I buy you a rum cock,
will you hold it against me?*
SEEN IN KOREA.

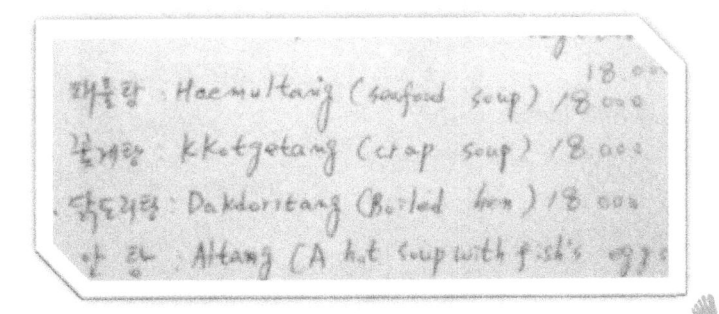

*Waiter, can you send this soup back?
It tastes like crap.*
SEEN IN KOREA.

66 Letchworth

> Please, urine only. This urinal is trying to watch its figure.
> SEEN IN KOREA.

> More like 18+
> SEEN IN KOREA.

14

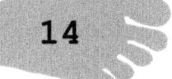

Haiku Hate
독도 또는 다케시마

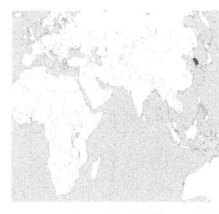

Korea's relationship with Japan is… complicated.

Imperial Japan occupied the Korean peninsula from 1910 until 1945, when Fat Man and Little Boy atomized Hiroshima and Nagasaki and the Japanese Empire finally surrendered.

The Koreans have never gotten over the 35-year occupation. Perhaps they never will. Japan issues apology after apology, and each time Korea responds with, "Not good enough."

In fact, check out a map from anywhere in the world, and the body of water between these two countries is labelled the "Sea of Japan." But look at a Korean map and it's called the "East Sea." As in, the sea which is EAST of KOREA. As in, the "Sea of KOREA."

The focal point of this nationalism is a territorial dispute over a tiny group of islands in the aforementioned "Sea of Japan/East Sea." These 46 acres of bald, barren rock are what the Japanese call Takeshima. But the Koreans call it Dokdo. The propaganda campaign surrounding Dokdo is intensive. From murals to documentary videos that play in loops on Korean subway screens, they really want you to know that Dokdo is, and always has been, Korean.

I don't think the Japanese are very bothered about Takeshima/Dokdo. But if you're in Korea, I believe that referring to it as Takeshima will promptly land you in a re-education camp, forced to sew Korean flags for the remainder of your days.

The rivalry between the countries persists into the present day, and enmity against the Japanese is handed down like an inheritance to the children of Korea.

I would like to share a few poems. My first poem is a Haiku entitled "Ode to Disgruntled Neighbors."

Children's hearts so pure
Filled with hate from history
Good grief, let it go

When teaching my fifth-grade Korean students a lesson on poetry, I figured the easiest introduction would be Haiku. The simple format for Haiku is: a 5-syllable line followed by a 7-syllable line and ending with a 5-syllable line.

Haiku is from Japan... Oops.

The sweetest, shyest girl in the class balled her little hands into fists and banged them against her knees, shouting, "Teacher! Hate Japan!"

All the other children joined in, howling curses about "Dokdo! Dokdo!" while jumping up and down on their chairs like it was the daily "Two Minutes of Hate" from a dystopian novel.

My second poem is also a Haiku. It is entitled "There Will Be Order in the Classroom."

Settle the Heck down!
I don't care about Dokdo
We're writing Haiku

Whenever precious vacation time popped up on the school calendar, I would often choose to visit Japan for the three or four days we were allotted. I mean, it's right next door. Just across the aforementioned "Sea of Japan/East Sea."

My Korean colleagues would attempt to dissuade me from going across the Sea-Which-Must-Not-Be-Named. My boss, Mr. Kim, was particularly passionate about this. Once, hearing that I planned to visit Osaka over the weekend, he cornered me and presented a litany of reasons why I should stay away from Japan.

"Sooo… The Japan have a many earthquake."

"Okay."

"Sooo… The Japan have a poison fish from the nuclear."

"Okay."

"Sooo… The Japan have the deadly mosquito."

"Okay."

And, when he ran out of semi-logical excuses: "Sooo… The Japan is the island. Maybe sink."

"You know what Mr Kim? I'll take my chances."

I'd like to close with a Haiku entitled "No Offense."

I enjoy Japan
Don't pretend it's not cooler
Sorry Korea

15

Karaoke in Japan
カラオケへの死

In America, you can stumble into any dive bar on a Tuesday night, scribble your name and "Sweet Caroline" onto a slip of paper, and see how many beers you can drink before it's your turn to make a fool of yourself on stage.

In Japan, karaoke is not sung in public. It is a private affair, as it should be.

Japan has special karaoke facilities where you can rent a sound-proof room and make a fool of yourself in front of your friends.

That's right — in Japan, you actually pay to sing karaoke. And to hear other people sing karaoke.

I think America should adopt this policy. In fact, I am starting a petition for a karaoke tax here in the States: If you break the rules and sing karaoke in a public place, you must pay $5 in cash to every person within earshot of your drunken Neil Diamond impression (*So good! So good! So good!*).

Karaoke, of course, is a Japanese word. Like tsunami. Like kamikaze. And every bit as horrifying.

A group of us travelled to Tokyo, the heart of karaoke country, a few years ago.

As sometimes occurs in the sloshy hours of a weekend night in the big city — when everyone should just go home to the capsule hotel and wake up the next day to a spilled beer that has flooded their tiny sleeping compartment — the group instead comes up with some variation on a terrible idea to stay out longer:

Hey, let's see how much raw squid we can eat before we puke!

Hey, let's all buy matching kimonos and get kicked out of a Japanese night club!

Hey, let's go sing karaoke!

So off we paraded to the place where they do that. We rented a dingy little room outfitted with a couple microphones, a flat screen, and a few dumpy couches. I have a vague memory of me and my friends screaming Neil Diamond lyrics (*So bad! So bad! So bad!*) before we all promptly passed out. When we woke up the next morning, we were presented with the bill. They had charged us by the hour. Good thing there were four of us to split it. At least it was cheaper than the kimonos.

The word karaoke, by the way, is Japanese for *kara,* which means "ear drum," and *oke,* which means "to make bleed."

16

Local Wildlife: VeniZEN
禅仏教の鹿のスープ

One of my favorite touring loops in the whole world is on the southern part of Japan's main island of Honshu. Start in Osaka, then on to Kyoto, to Kobe, to Nara, and then back to Osaka. I enjoy Osaka for the Blade Runner neon lights and night life of the concrete jungle metropolis; Kyoto for the relaxing Zen beauty of temple grounds; Kobe for the steak; and Nara for the… deer?

I'm from the American South. Deer don't impress me. On the road they're a hazard, in the woods they're a meal.

But the Nara deer have the distinction of being strict Buddhists, and this has a notable effect on their demeanor. Even the locals regard them as holy. Freely roaming the temple grounds, they are cute, approachable, and they love to be hand-fed. They even bow in honorific fashion before accepting food. The good ones, anyway.

They're not limited to eating out of the palm of your hand. Some will prance up and sniff around your person to see if you're hiding any goodies in your pockets.

I had just been to the ATM, which had spit out a couple of 5,000 Yen notes (about $50 US each). I had shoved them both in my back pocket, not worried about pickpockets in Japan.

A deer approached me. I offered it crackers. As she bowed before me to humbly accept my offering, I felt a forceful nudge on my behind. I spun around, but not quickly enough. The molester made off with one of my Yen notes, chomping it in three bites until there was nothing left.

"Oi! What the hell, Bambi?! You know what we do with you back home, right?"

She just stared at me with those big doe eyes.

"You know how many fistfuls of crackers I could have bought you with that 5,000 Yen note?"

She winked at me, tossed her head and gamboled away. Perhaps she was trying to teach me some Zen lesson about the ephemeral nature of material things.

But if she had pulled that move back home in the Ozark mountains, she'd have found herself the featured ingredient in my chili that night.

17

Zeros Matter
私はあなたの神戸牛を愛し

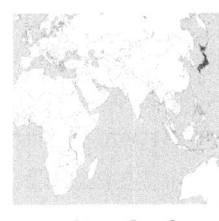

I am cheap. I will haggle over pennies until we're both red in the face. I'll walk a mile to save a buck on bus fare.

Remember — being cheap equals traveling farther.

My dinner plans in Asia usually consist of hitting up a couple street-food vendors to the tune of maybe two bucks total.

But I do treat myself, on occasion. Such an occasion presented itself in Kobe, Japan.

Kobe beef comes from the most prized cows in the world. If you've been to a restaurant in America, and you think you've had Kobe beef — you haven't.

The Japanese jealously guard the Kobe brand.

Gastropubs are being sued for calling their mini-burgers "Kobe Sliders." Restaurants erroneously boasting that their Texas prime beef is "Kobe" are just asking for a cease-and-desist letter from a Japanese law firm.

Kobe beef isn't just about cow-breeding. True Kobe beef is all about the tradition of cow-pampering. The Japanese pamper their cows more than the Queen pampers the royal corgi litter. A Kobe cow gets massaged daily, fed only the choicest of feed, and even drinks beer from the bottle. (Most Asian beer is bull piss. Japanese beer? Surprisingly good.)

The Japanese are just crackerjack at perfecting, well, everything. Kobe beef is a shining example of that dedication to quality.

The desk guy at the Japanese hostel recommended a place to enjoy an authentic Kobe steak. He typed the Google-Maps location into my phone. I walked past rows of wooden houses with sliding doors, past Torii gate arches of Shinto shrines. When I arrived at the place, I had to double-check the GPS coordinates. The restaurant was very unassuming. It looked like a casual sandwich shop — wooden stools, tile floor, people in t-shirts.

I grabbed a stool at a high table and checked out the single-page laminated menu.

Now, I'd had a steak on a recent jaunt to Tokyo, and it came out to about $30 US. At the conversion rate that was, what — 30,000 Japanese Yen, right? So when I saw a Kobe Steak for 20,000 Yen, I jumped on it. A $20 Kobe steak? Yes, please. Hostel guy had steered me in the right direction.

It came out ten minutes after I ordered it. It was a fist-sized petite, all of six ounces, and had already been cut up into bite-sized cubes of medium-rare. I decided to forget about my grilling philosophy of "keep the juice inside the meat, don't you dare cut into it" and trust that the Japanese know what they're doing.

Boy howdy, do they ever. Each bite melted like butter onto my tongue and exploded in little flavor-bombs. To this day, it is the single best thing I have ever put into my mouth. The hype had been lived up to. And for only 20,000 Yen!

I wasn't full, but for the price, I was satisfied. I'd finally tasted the legendary Kobe.

I walked to the lunch counter to pay. "Do you speak English?" I asked the girl.

"Yes, okay, little bit."

"Well," I said, "my compliments to the chef. That was the best steak I have ever eaten in my entire life. I will still be tasting it for years to come."

"Yes," she smiled. "Thank you."

"Domo Arigato to you!" I beamed. "So, how much do I owe you?"

She pulled up my ticket and dinged the cash register. "Twenty thousand Yen."

"Deal," I said, and pulled out my wallet. I still had US currency I needed to get rid of. "You wouldn't by any chance accept US dollars, would you?"

"Yes. Okay."

"Great!" I handed her a twenty dollar bill with an honorific bow.

"Oh," she said, "So sorry. Not enough."

"Ah," I said, pulling out a couple of dollar bills. "I guess the conversion isn't exact. What is it? Twenty-*two* dollars?"

"No," she said, handing me back the twenty. "This only two thousand Yen."

I grabbed the menu off the counter and meditated on that number under "Kobe Steak." Twenty thousand…

Oh. Oh God no. It can't possibly be.

I'd been living in Korea for the past 6 months and had adapted to the currency conversion. One dollar equals 1,000 Korean Won. The rule of thumb is: add three zeros to the number — $20 US is about 20,000 Korean Won.

But for the Japanese Yen, you only add two zeros to arrive at an approximate conversion rate. I had counted my zeros all wrong.

"Are you telling me this is a two-hundred-dollar steak?"

"Twenty thousand Yen," she repeated, matching the expression of worry I was wearing on my face.

As I continued staring at the menu, she shouted in the direction of the kitchen. When I looked up, I was surrounded by every employee at the restaurant.

"Whoa, hey," I said, throwing up my hands, "I'm not going to run. I just… Two hundred dollars?"

Everyone who had created a perimeter around me was Japanese, except one man in a chef hat and apron who appeared to be of Indian descent.

"Wait, who are you then?" I blurted out to him.

"I'm the head chef," he said.

"Are you from…"

"India, my friend." He wagged his head. "Near the border of Nepal."

"Are you… Hindu?"

He cocked his head. "Yes? And?"

"So lemme get this straight. You're a Hindu — a religion that worships cows — and you're the head chef at a Kobe beef restaurant? I'm so confused right now."

"We really need you to pay for your steak, sir."

I pulled my wallet back out. "Ok. Here's the deal. I'm an honest man, I'm not going to skip out on this bill, which I can't even believe right now. But if this card doesn't work, somebody is going to have to go to an ATM with me."

The card worked. I ducked out of the restaurant and made a beeline back to the hostel to have a little chat with the desk guy who had recommended the joint, the taste of the most expensive steak in the world still on my tongue.

I couldn't afford a massage now if I wanted to. Even beer was out of my budget for the next few days.

But somewhere, a Kobe cow was getting a drunken rub-down.

I had paid $200. Ol' Bessie would pay the ultimate price.

18

Grandma's Kimchi Recipe
할머니의 김치를 먹어

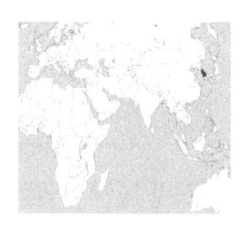

Don't go to Korea if you don't like kimchi, or you'll starve. I love the stuff, and I miss it every day I'm away. The stinky staple is the "Heart and Seoul" of the Korean diet. It's in everything. Soups. Salads. Doughnuts. It's served with everything. Lunch. Dinner. Breakfast!

This fermented cabbage dish is a time-tested cure for a variety of ailments, dontcha know — from carpal tunnel to cancer — even chlamydia (according to a friend).

Korean homes even have a special, separate kimchi fridge, because the overpowering aroma will permeate all foods within proximity. The old timers just throw it in pots and bury them in the backyard for the winter, like squirrels with acorns.

Every family has a kimchi recipe. The following recipe is an ancient secret which I was able to wrest from an old hunchbacked woman on the streets of Seoul after pumping her with *soju* rice wine. You're welcome.

The process of kimchi-making as told to me by the old woman sounds extremely sensual. Or maybe she was just hitting on me. I'll let you decide.

You will need:

- Normal-sized tub
- X-Large tub
- Rubber gloves (to keep the ingredients from burning off layers of your skin)
- Clay pots for backyard burying
- Numerous heads of Napa cabbage
- Coarse salt
- Kimchi paste ingredients
- More coarse salt

1. Cradle each cabbage head in your hands and, one by one, tenderly open them up like a lotus flower. (*Cue candlelight.*)
2. Gently place the deflowered cabbage heads in a tub.
3. Soothingly massage their leaves with salt. (*Cue mood music.*)
4. Add more salt. Keep massaging.
5. Continue massaging until all the cabbage heads are fully relaxed and emitting moisture. (*Bow chicka wow wow.*)
6. Carefully squeeze excess moisture from the leaves.

7. In a separate tub, mix together the following ingredients until they form a paste:
   - 1 cup red pepper flakes
   - 1 tablespoon salt
   - 2 tablespoons sugar
   - 2 tablespoons oyster sauce
   - 5 tablespoons fish sauce
   - 7 tablespoons fish-out-of-water sauce
   - 2-inch piece of ginger root
   - The square root of 4,238
   - 2 bulbs of garlic, cloves separated and peeled
   - 2 young gazelles, cloven hooves separated and peeled
   - 1 handful teeny tiny dehydrated minnows
   - 1 handful teeny tiny dehydrated sea-monkeys
   - 1 vial dragon's blood
   - 1 teaspoon mermaid scale shavings
   - 3 droplets vestal virgin tears
   - 4 egg-whites of a griffin
   - 4 egg-yolks of Kathy Griffin
   - 5 golden rings
   - And a partridge in a pear tree

8. Take each relaxed head of cabbage and rub in the kimchi paste, starting gently from the center and massaging outward in a circular motion until completely slathered. (*It was at this point that the old woman took my hand and massaged it gently. Still not sure if she was just demonstrating or hitting on me. Let the reader decide.*)
9. Transfer to a pot. Cover. Bury in ground for 87 winters.

While you wait for your kimchi to mature, head down to any Korean restaurant and eat as much of it as your heart desires. Right there off the *banchan* line. Just pile it on your plate, no one cares. In Korea, kimchi is free.

19

#TeachingInKorea
열심히 공부하다

I never once set my alarm for the eighteen months I taught English in Seoul. The classes at the after-school English academy didn't begin until 4 p.m. Korea was my first experience teaching ESL (English as a Second Language) abroad. My original contract was for twelve months. I liked it enough to stick around for another six. I guess I just couldn't quit the kimchi.

#Teacher-Teacher

In Korea, "Sam" is the title for teacher. They use it after your first name:

Jack-Sam.
Jill-Sam.
John Jacob Jingleheimer Schmidt-Sam.

I am Sam-Sam.
Sam-Sam I am.

#WouldYouLikeRiceWithThat

"What's your favorite food?" I always ask a class of Korean students on getting-to-know-you day. More often than not it goes like this:

"Rice."

"Rice and...?"

"Rice."

"Rice with soy sauce on it?"

"Rice."

"Just a bowl of bland, white rice, huh?"

"Rice."

#DancingEyebrows

I can do the wave with my eyebrows. It must be some genetically recessive trait I inherited that allows me to move each eyebrow independently. When my students are taking a test, I like to break out this trick.

A student will look up from their test, as if to search the air for the answer. When his eyes drift over to me, I'll do the eyebrows.

"Whoa!" he'll exclaim in the silence, and the rest of the class will raise their heads.

"Teacher, do it again!" he'll demand.

"Do what?"

"The eyebrows!"

Then he'll try to replicate the trick in hilarious fashion, succeeding only in making his eyes wide and rolling them up into his sockets. The rest of the class will be entirely confused.

"Get back to work," I'll tell him.

He'll huff and puff, and look back up every minute for the rest of the test. And I'll just smile and point at the paper in front of him.

I've got to amuse myself somehow.

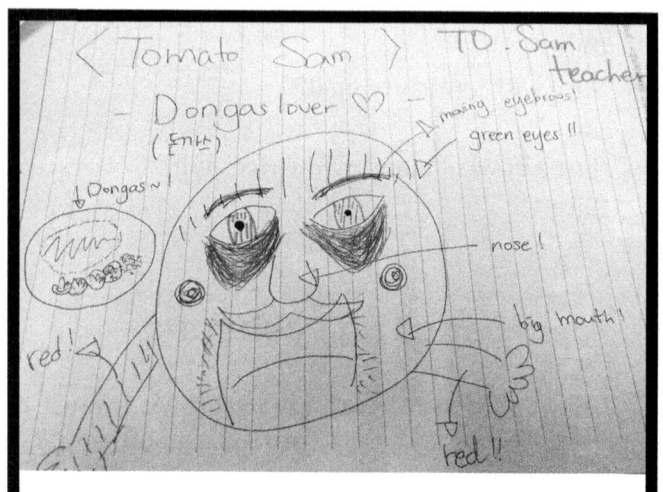

A rather unflattering caricature of yours truly. Note the detail paid to my "moving eyebrows." Also, my big mouth, red complexion, and affinity for Dongas (Korean for *Katsudon*, which I explore in Chapter 35). This must have been a Monday. The kids always commented on the dark circles under my eyes on Mondays.

#YosemiteSam

One of my students traveled to American National Parks during summer break. She gave me this very thoughtful personalized souvenir from Yosemite (which this fourth-grade Korean girl could pronounce correctly, unlike the 45th president of the United States).

As a matter of perfect coincidence, she wasn't even aware of Yosemite Sam — that wild, swashbuckling adversary of Bugs Bunny.

Yessirree! I'm the hootin'est, tootin'est English teacher 'round these parts!

#*TreeIrishTrees*

As the Head Teacher at a Korean English Academy, one of my responsibilities was to observe the other teachers and give them notes.

An English teacher had just come to us from Ireland. Keith. (Or as he pronounced it, "Keet.") He was a great guy, and I endeared myself to him immediately. We drank beer in the evenings after school, and traveled together to Japan and Southeast Asia whenever our schedule allowed. The Irish are the most entertaining and true-blue friends you can hope to meet. Keith was no exception.

Of all the classes I could have sat in on, Keith's elementary school lesson this day was on numbers. I pulled up a chair in the back, pad and pencil in hand. Keith was fine, and this was a formality. I would much rather have been eating kimchi jiggae at the local Kimbab Cheonguk with this hour of my time, but hey, that's why they paid me the big bucks — to watch Keith teach Korean kids how to count and tell him, hey, you're doing fine, of course. Cheers to the beers this evening, mate!

"How many trees do you see in the picture?" Keith asked the class.

I had almost dozed off. I looked over at the open book of the student nearest me. There were three trees on the page.

A boy with glasses and a bowl-cut in the front row shot his hand up.

"Yes, Dexter?" Keith said, calling on the boy. (The kids pick their own English names, mostly after soccer stars or Disney princesses. Young Dexter was obviously a precocious fan of the serial killer genre.)

"Tuh-lee tuh-lees-uh!" Dexter proclaimed smugly.

"Tat's right!" boomed Keith in his thick Irish brogue. "I see *tree* trees! Say it with me everybody! I. See. *Tree.* Trees!"

The class echoed in unison. "Ah-ee. See. Tuh-lee. Tuh-lees-uh!"

"One, two, *tree* trees!"

"One, two, tuh-lee tuh-lees-uh!" the class responded.

"Great job, class!" Keith beamed, quite proud of his kids. "And now turn in your books to page turty-two."

I had to leave the room, I was laughing so hard.

#Furt

I gave the fifth grade class an essay prompt:

Describe an embarrassing situation.

This student's essay was so inspiring that I had to take a photo before handing it back.

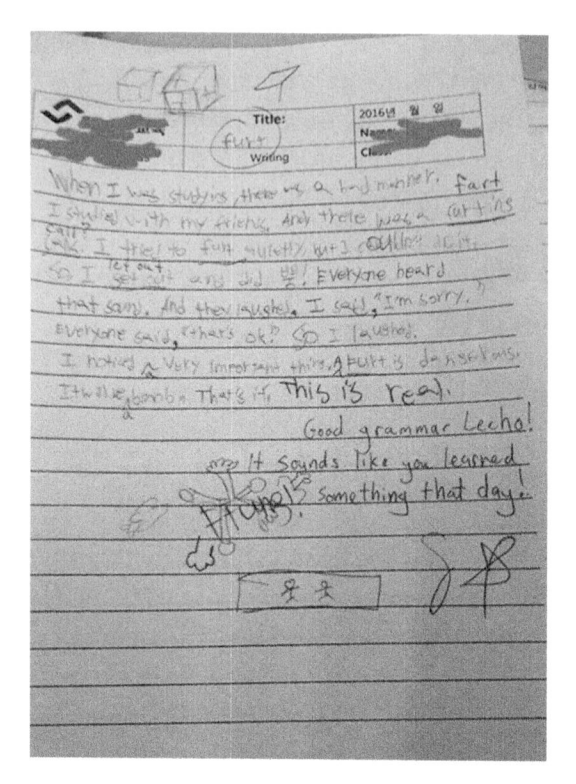

Here's the transcript.

Title: Furt

When I was studying, there was a bad manner. I studied with my friends. And, there was a furting. I tried to furt quietly, but I couldn't do it. So, I let it out and did BBOONG! [The student notated this sound in the Korean Hangeul.] Everyone heard that sound. And they laughed. I said, 'I'm sorry.' Everyone said, 'That's OK.' So I laughed. I noticed a very important thing. A furt is dangerous. It will be a bomb. That's it. THIS IS REAL.

20

Just the Way You Are
당신은 이미 아름답습니다

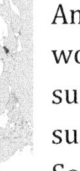

An estimated one in three Korean women have some form of cosmetic surgery before they turn 29. I suspect more.

South Korea is the plastic surgery capital of the world, making Seoul the Mecca of nip and tuck.

I gave a classroom of teenage Korean girls an essay assignment:

> *If I had a million dollars*
> *(1 billion Won)*
> *to spend in one day, I would...*

The girls wrote furiously. When they had finished, I called on them one by one to read their essays aloud. Every single girl, all twelve of them, said the same thing.

"If I had a million dollars,

I would: Fix. My. Face."

As though there were something wrong with it!

The most common cosmetic procedure is called a blepharoplasty. Many Koreans have a genetic trait referred to as a "monolid," or an eyelid without a crease. A blepharoplasty, (or "double-eyelid surgery") widens the eyes and makes them appear... well, more Western.

It just snowballs from there. Next comes the nose job, then the chin, then the jaw bones, until the patient's facial features are that of a harsh Cubist portrait.

And if you've already gone all-in on the face, you've probably earned a coupon for a new set of boobs.

Society encourages this image disorder. You are more likely to be hired if your face meets the fake aesthetic that is being pushed by advertisements and K-Pop culture.

For a people that are fiercely proud of their heritage and ethnicity, the Koreans sure are quick to cast a surgery-widened eye down upon the phenotypic expression of their genes. Parents routinely buy their daughters new eyes and noses for graduation. Young women will publicly and proudly display the bandages over their faces like badges of honor.

I looked out over the classroom in disbelief. These poor girls. Had they never been told that they were pretty? I took it upon myself.

"All of you are beautiful," I said with sincerity, "just the way you are."

They rolled their eyes.

At least I tried.

21

SPAM Donor
시계 몬티 파이썬

On major holidays, Koreans give each other gift baskets. Not fruit. Not gourmet chocolates. Not wine and cheese baskets either. They give the gift that keeps on giving, year after year: SPAM.

No, this is not a Monty Python sketch.

During national festivals like Cheusok (Korean Thanksgiving), and Solnal (the Chinese Lunar New Year), the grocery stores in Korea turn into a national SPAM convention. Aisles and aisles of baskets and boxes are on display and stacked to the ceiling with lovely, wonderful SPAM!

Cue the Vikings! (A Viking chorus emerges from Aisle 3, chanting, "SPAM, SPAM, SPAMITTY SPAM")

> For every woman, child and man,
> There is a flavor of SPAM in a can!
> SPAM *Classic* is one that cannot be resisted,
> It's been around before your grandpa existed!
> You've recently had a high blood pressure test?
> Try *Low Sodium* SPAM — 25 percent less!
> And how 'bout you sonny, are you feeling fat?
> You can still enjoy SPAM *Lite* — how about that!?
> *Hot and Spicy*, *Mezclita*, and *Jalapeño*,
> And a dozen delicious SPAM flavors to go!
> Now with *Real Bacon*! With *Garlic*, with *Cheese*!
> Now in *Singles* and *Patties* —or *Spread* if you please!
> If your tongue wants to taste a new style of meat,
> There's an *Oven Roast Turkey* SPAM! Wow, what a treat!
> *Hickory Smoke* wins my blue ribbon prize,
> And get this — there's even SPAM breaded *French Fries*!
> If you like spice, why, try the new seasoned stuff!
> With *Tocino*, *Chorizo* — there's never enough!
> The *Portuguese Sausage* is sure to impress
> *Teriyaki*, *Black Pepper*... Ah, but I digress.

To every woman, child, and man:
Come down to Korea, and pick out your can
Of SPAM SPAM SPAMITTY SPAAAM!

I didn't make up any of those twenty SPAM varieties, by the way. Not even the french fries.

By the end of my 18-month tenure in Seoul, I must've received about three dozen tins of gifted SPAM. They sat in the corner of my kitchen, collecting dust. (Although, once when I was in the mood to cook "Something Completely Different," I was tempted to pop open a can in order to make *Lobster Thermidor aux crevettes with a Mornay sauce, served in a Provencale manner with shallots and aubergines, garnished with truffle pâté, brandy and a fried egg on top — and SPAM.*)

SPAM has been incorporated into contemporary Korean cuisine. The most popular example is a dish called *budae jjigae*. The fixin's are as follows:

- Ramen. Out of the packet.
- Kimchi. Which is practically falling from the sky in Korea.
- Hot dogs. Not bratwurst or a sturdy, smoked sausage, but the teenie-weenies that come out of a can.
- The main ingredient, of course: SPAM.

If you sourced these fraternity house cupboard ingredients and cooked them at home, I'm betting it would run you $3, maybe $4 US for a chili pot's worth to feed a crew of hungry frat boys.

There are restaurants in Korea that specialize in *budae jjigae*. Guess how much they charge per person? The equivalent of Nine. Dollars. The kicker? They make you cook it yourself! Each table has a large, built-in steel bowl. Fire up the gas heater underneath and cook your own damn Ramen 'n SPAM. Toss a couple slices of plastic cheese on top, and bon appétit!

I was already familiar with this dish long before coming to Korea. I have cooked *budae jjigae* (aka *found-it-in-the-fridge-at-3am*) during my college days. I remember (vaguely) leaning on the open fridge door and doing a desperate inventory. "What have we got to eat? Some ramen, a couple of hot dogs, plastic cheese, condiments… and an old can of SPAM."

Which is exactly how budae jjigae was conceived. Not by a hungry, drunk bachelor, but by starving civilians in a war-ravaged Korea throwing together anything they could find. In the aftermath of the Korean War in 1953, food was scarce, and the people scrounged U.S. Army bases for canned and preserved food. Some

SPAM discarded by an American soldier was a golden tin of sustenance to a starving Korean. Hence the name *budae jjigae*, or "army stew."

With such myriad and amazing Korean dishes out there, it seems insane to settle for budae jjigae.

Perhaps this remnant of a desperate era serves as a point of nostalgia. A memory of a time that should not be forgotten, of a war that persists to this day, divorcing the Korean peninsula and the people from each other.

Maybe what those angry North Koreans need, now more than ever, is a gift box. Of Lovely. Wonderful. SPAM.

I'll be happy to donate mine.

22

Et Tu, Taxi Traitor?!
เมืองแห่งหัวขโมย

It was my first time in Bangkok. For my inaugural night in *Good Time City*, I figured I should check out the infamous Khao San Road. This backpacker party street is in the Old Town, and my hostel was miles away across the sprawling metropolis.

I bought a Leo beer at one of the half-dozen 7-Elevens within sight and waved down a taxi. I hopped in the backseat passenger side.

"Sawat dee, hello. Khao San Road," I said, and cracked open my beer. "It's okay if I drink?"

The cabbie turned around, and nodded his head. We rode down the congested streets of Bangkok, past the illuminated stupas of Buddhist temples and the endless green-red-orange parade of 7-Elevens.

"Okay if I smoke?"

He turned around again. "Window," he said, motioning me to roll it down with the classic crank handle. As I did, he mimed puffing a cigarette and pointed to himself. I handed him a Marlboro.

We both lit up. I got out my phone and typed Khao San Road into Google Maps. I followed the movement of the blue GPS dot. Something was amiss. We were heading away from the destination.

"Are we going the right way?"

"Shortcut," he said, puffing away.

"I hope you're not running up the meter, just because I'm a farang." (*Farang* is foreigner in Thai.) "I gave you a cigarette, man."

We slowed to a stop. I threw my head out the window to see a police road block ahead. Royal Thai police officers were shining flashlights into stopped cars. My driver waved his hand out the window, Marlboro Red still burning between his fingers.

I chugged my Leo and tossed my cigarette butt into the bottle so as not to litter or, worse, pay a hefty fine for littering. The officers came to our car. They stood on either side of the taxi, shining their torches directly into my eyes.

My driver was chatting up the cop on his side. They were both laughing.

"Get out," said the other officer, opening my door.

He was wearing aviator sunglasses. It was ten o'clock at night. "Has there been a terror attack?" I asked. The Erawan Shrine in Bangkok was bombed just a few months before.

He didn't answer. He took me to a fold-out table that was set up on the sidewalk. There were two chairs. He took one.

"Sit," he said. "Passport."

I sat down, and produced my American passport. He flipped through it and set it on the table. He handed me a laminated page filled with paragraphs in all different languages. He ran his finger down past French, Chinese, Spanish, and landed on the English.

"You. Read," he ordered.

I cleared my throat.

> ```
> It is prohibited for the
> operator of a motor vehicle to
> consume alcohol or tobacco at
> any time.
> ```

"Look, I'm sorry I gave the driver a cigarette, I didn't know the law —"

The officer pointed to the next line.

> ```
> This also applies to any and
> all passengers.
> ```

"Great." I read the last line slowly.

> ```
> The offense is punishable by 6
> months jail time and/or a fine
> of 20,000 Baht.
> ```

The ground gave out from under me. I was dizzy, my heart sank into my stomach, and I had the sudden urge to throw up.

"Please don't do this to me," I gulped.

"We go police station," replied the cop.

I folded my hands in supplication. "I beg you, please don't do this to me. What about the driver?!"

"No care about him."

I stared in disbelief at the words. "20,000 Baht." I did the math in my head. "That's like $650 dollars!"

"We go police station."

It was a shakedown. My driver had deliberately taken me to this police checkpoint. He had sold me out, and I was at the mercy of the Royal Thai Police.

The cop and I just sat there, him with his crossed arms and mirrored sunglasses, me with my head in my hands replaying every episode of "Locked Up Abroad" in my mind.

And we sat. And sat some more. He didn't seem in a rush to "go police station." Hopefully there would be someone there with better English and a little sympathy. Maybe I would be able to pay my way out of this before I get hooked and booked — Heeey, wait a minute...

I had just broken a 1,000 Baht note buying that ill-fated bottle of beer. That would still only be about $30 US, but it was all the cash I'd brought. Worth a shot.

I reached into my pocket. I dropped the fistful of bills onto the plastic table. The officer quickly threw his hat on top of the pile, *Godfather II*-style. He handed me my passport. "Go," he said.

I folded my hands in gratitude. "Khob khun khap," I said, thanking him.

I walked down the street in a cool wave of relief, then split the scene as fast as I could, should these dirty cops decide I hadn't given them enough bribe money.

"Oi! Mate!" came a voice from across the road. A burly white guy with a fu manchu mustache and a

Hawaiian shirt two sizes too small was waving me down. "Hold up then!" He strutted across the busy street with no regard for the traffic.

"I saw the whole thing," he said in a thick Australian accent. "How'd they pinch ya?"

"Cabbie screwed me," I said, and kept walking. "Turned me over to the cops for an open beer and a cigarette, which I even bummed him one, which is apparently illegal."

"This upside-down town, mate," he said, matching my stride. "Rip-off City. How much was the backhand?"

"The what?"

"The bribe! What did you pay them?"

"1,000 Baht. All I had."

"Whew! Lucky bloke, you. These jellybacks they got here'll grease you for heaps more. He was in a good mood. Wife must've done him a good gobby this morning. More than I can say for meself, aye aye aye!" He thrust out his hand. "Simon." He smiled, revealing a large section of missing teeth on the right side of his mouth.

"Sam," I said, and shook his hand. We kept walking.

"Yeh, yeh, they'll do you a mischief here, Sam. Do it with a smile. Bloody hell, I got nicked this one time —"

He was interrupted by the cabbie, who was running after us, shouting "My meter! You pay me!"

"Whoa whoa whoa!" Simon stopped and held out his hands. "Settle petal! What's your fuss then, ya cheeky derro?"

I stopped too. I felt strangely as though I was in good hands.

I should mention that there was a lot of *c-word* peppered heavily throughout everything that came out of

Simon's mouth. Out of ANY Aussie's mouth, for that matter. Those Australians and their beloved *c-word*.

The cabbie turned his ire onto me. "You pay!" he shouted.

"Whinge whinge, you shonky sook," said Simon, and lit a cigarette. "Go get your cut from your copper friends."

"You sold me out, man," I contributed. "You drove me straight to this police checkpoint. Why did you do that to me?"

"You pay now!" The cabbie waved his fist, spitting curses at us. He had "lost face," as they say in Thailand. It's very rare when a Thai loses face. And very bad. Very, very bad.

Simon was unphased. He leaned into the man and whispered, "Have another durry, mate." With that, he flicked his lit cigarette directly into the cabbie's chest. "Now piss off."

The cabbie bared his teeth.

Simon turned round and shoved me. "Tear ass, mate! Go go go!"

We took off running down the street. We rounded the first corner, straight into the bright lights of 7-Eleven.

"Behind the Sevie!" Simon cried, pushing me into the alley behind the building. We stood there panting with our backs pressed against the wall.

A few moments later, the cabbie ran past us down the street.

Simon pulled my shirt collar. "Inside!" he whisper-shouted.

I followed him into the 7-Eleven. The sliding doors went *ding* and we made a beeline for the cooler in the back. We crouched down, catching our breath.

Simon opened the beer fridge door. "Have a cold one about it." He grabbed a bottle of Leo.

"That's bad luck beer," I said, peering up over the snack food aisle to see if we'd been followed.

"Stay down, mate," said Simon, and pushed me down by my shoulders. He pulled two green bottles from the bottom rung and passed one to me. "Here's a Chang, then. That's a decent stubby. Cheaper anyway."

"How much cheaper?"

"40 Baht versus 36."

I dug into my pocket and fished for any straggling coins. I spread them out on my hand. There were exactly three 10 Baht coins, one 5 Baht coin, and a 1 Baht coin.

"Thirty-six!" I exclaimed, like I had just won Bingo.

"Aren't you the luckiest [c-word] in the Land of Smiles! Come on then." He slapped my arm and rose to his feet. "Let's get outta here."

"Where to?"

Simon took a long swig of his Chang beer. "You ever see a ping-pong show?"

"No?"

"It's incredible what these sheilas can do with their [c-word]'s. My treat, mate. My treat."

23

Gaspers, Grumblers, Snufflers, and Snorters
กรนทุกคน

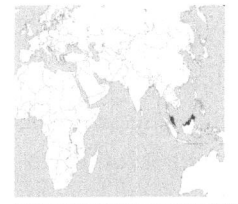

Important Public Service Announcement: If you can't fall asleep to people snoring, you shouldn't be staying in hostels.

Sorry. Because, guess what? EVERYBODY SNORES.

So if you are a delicate sleeper and haven't learned how to sleep comfortably with earplugs, don't be jealous that others around you are getting some good shut-eye. Spring for a private room.

I have encountered true champions of gravel-grinding in my travels. I have shared bunk beds with gaspers, grumblers, snufflers, and snorters.

Expect that these corn-crackers will be in the bed next to you, and plan accordingly.

And I've got news for you. You snore. Oh, you think you don't? When you have one of those late nights on the town and stumble back to the hostel in the wee hours of the morning, collapsing stone-drunk backwards onto the bottom bunk — believe me, you will saw logs with the best of them.

My own snoring has been described as cartoonish. A faintly rumbling inhale, and a whistling exhale, a feather hovering above my face blowing up and down with every metered breath.

I was hanging out in Penang, a Malaysian island in the Strait of Malacca near the Thai border. After a full day of temple-chasing, I had dined on the island's famed dish, Laksa. One bowl of those sweet-and-sour fish noodles wasn't enough, so I had another. And another. Three bowls put me down for the count, and I retired early.

I awoke abruptly to being poked in the chest. The culprit was an older gentleman, which is rare in youth hostels, but not completely out of the ordinary. This European fellow (we don't need to say which country he was from, but it rhymes with Nance) was punching his finger into my pectoral.

"Can I help you?"

"You are the snorer," he said sternly. "No one in this room can sleep."

"Oh really? Did you take a poll?"

"You must stop the snoring," he demanded.

"You must get *on-up-out-my-face* right now," I said, sitting up in bed, "or we're going to make the front page of the Malaysian Star tomorrow."

"Trou du cul Américain," he grunted, and stormed back to his bed.

"Hey! I know what that means, asshole!" I shouted back.

At 3 a.m., a guy stumbled into the room after having very obviously drunk all the rum in Penang. He climbed into the bunk directly above my "new best friend" and proceeded to call the hogs louder than anyone I'd ever heard. All. Night. Long.

When I got up to take a pee, I noticed our Monsieur was sitting straight up in bed, watching the bulge in the mattress above him sag and heave with every snore. I winked and whispered, "En Francais, comment dites-vous cela —Karma's a bitch, ain't it?"

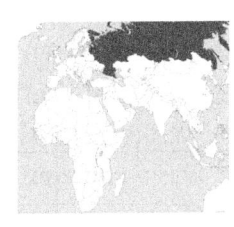

Okay. So, I know Russia isn't Asia. But I encountered the world heavyweight champion of snoring in a hostel in Moscow.

I remember waking with a start, convinced that the NAZI's were invading Russia all over again. I couldn't even be mad. It was so outrageous, I couldn't stop laughing. I busted out my phone and recorded the audio of this bomb-bursting coal-raker for when I might need a good chuckle on a long train ride.

"Mike," I whispered to my travelling buddy in the bunk below me. "You awake?"

"Oh yeah," he said at conversational volume. He also had his phone out and was recording the cacophony. We laid there, listening to Darth Vader having carnal relations with a B52 bomber. The howling, gasping, screaming copulation of machine on machine was anything but consensual.

> To hear my impersonation of the Russian snorer, get the audio-book version of this book.

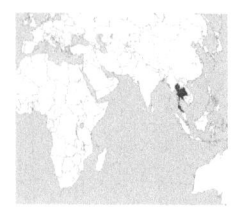

Once, on the tiny island of Koh Tao in the Gulf of Thailand, some fellow travelers and I made a full day of snorkeling those remote and glassy waters and soaking up sun. That evening, we grabbed beers and strolled along the beach. We skinny-dipped in the surf and lounged on the sand, laughing and carrying on to the sound of crashing waves under the full moon. Among our crew was a gorgeous German girl, Helga, who had enchanted me with her Alpine accent and shimmering sea-water eyes.

Being a crew assembled from the same dormitory room, we made our barefoot way back to the hostel, and all retired to our own beds.

I awoke to a vision of the fair maiden Helga. Indeed, she was in the bed with me, leaning over me, her hands on my chest, whispering, "Psst. Saaaaammmm. Psst."

Half asleep, I assumed what any man would naturally assume if a beautiful German girl was rousing him softly in the middle of the night.

"Hey, Fraulein," I smiled dreamily, and wrapped my arms around her.

"Sam. You are sound like zee bear. In zee cave."

Damn. Think fast, you slumbering fool. "Well Helga, two bears can fit in this cave."

"You can roll over, yes?"

"Anything for you, my Germanic queen."

She smiled in approval, patted my face and went back to her bunk. I rolled over and had such fantastical dreams of romance in the Bavarian countryside that I must have snored louder than before dear Helga had awakened me.

24

HOSTEL
Bọ chét Nhà trọ

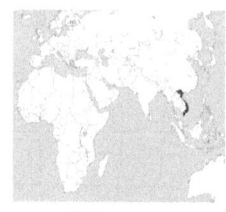

For half the price of an Egg McMuffin Meal, you can have: a Bed *AND* Breakfast *AND* Beer at a decent hostel in Hanoi. And, if you wake up early enough, a hot shower.

Whereas most hostels around the world will put out some toast and jam in the morning, in 'Nam you get a choice of: made-to-order eggs and toast, a banh mi sandwich, fried rice, or the most popular breakfast food in the land — phở. Pick a tea or a juice, but if you go with the local coffee, you'll be drinking the best in the world.

Hostels in Hanoi offer free beer in the evening, usually for one hour (or until they run out). One hostel may start pouring at 7 p.m., another at 8 p.m., and so on. Theoretically, one could go on a hostel-hopping "free beer tour." Hit every hostel lobby when their drinking hour commences, all the way until midnight, without spending a single Dong, (but you *will* pay for it in the form of donations at the porcelain altar the next morning).

This sounds too good to be true — and, to be fair, it is. The beer on offer is "Bia Hoi," which translates to "Fresh Beer." Ha! Now *that's* fresh. Bia Hoi is a quick-fermentation, lowest of the low-grade swill, and weighs in at about only 3% alcohol per volume. Though every batch of this near beer is different (the colder the better), the taste is what I would describe as an old banana that farted into a pressurized, metallic container. But if you drink the first three fast, you won't taste the next twelve.

RECEPTiON
Welcom turist we spik Inglish

SPOTTED IN A HOSTEL
IN DA NANG, VIETNAM.

These metal Bia Hoi containers are delivered daily in the form of dented beer kegs, stacked and strapped down on the backs of motorbikes. I've seen as many as six full-size kegs being couriered in this fashion at once.

Free Breakfast.
Free Beer.
And Free Bedbugs.

> *Good night.*
> *Sleep tight.*
> *Don't let the bedbugs bite.*

Bedbugs — the 8th Plague — are the bane of every backpacker's existence.

This isn't to say you can't catch bedbugs from any old guest bed, from the swanky to the scanty. But a living quarters housing a dozen fresh, warm bodies at a time, from all over the world, is the most ideal environment for a bed bug colony to flourish. It's all the right conditions for a perfect storm of pestilence.

You know you're a victim of the Cimex Lectularius when you awake to a series of inflamed, red bites in a striated pattern down your arm, your back, your leg. The infernal insect feeds on your flesh as it trails down a patch of skin, then, bloated with your blood, ambles away to a dark and quiet place — a nook in the wall, underneath a mattress, or... inside your backpack. They are resilient creatures, and can lie dormant for months without feeding, popping out eggs while they wait for the hunger to return.

This is why, when you discover the tell-tale signs of having been host to the parasite, you have to assume that they are burrowed in every seam and every fold of every corner of your belongings, where they have been busy laying hundreds of microscopic eggs.

People have different advice for getting rid of them, all of which involve the application of heat. Some say to throw your backpack and all your clothes into an industrial dryer set on high for hours. Some say that running a hair dryer on full heat inside and around your backpack will do the trick.

I am of the opinion that these insidious creatures are so hardy that, just short of burning everything, the heat of a clothes or hair dryer are going to seem like a beach vacation to the buggers.

At a hostel in Hanoi called the Funky Jungle (which is defunct now, actually bulldozed due to the infestation of bed bugs, which I doubt affected the survival of their colonies), I woke up with my back streaked with itchy red dots. I tried counting them in the mirror, my head craned around my shoulder, and lost count after 40. I tried all the hot dryers methods, but each night they continued to make a dinner of my soft, pink flesh.

Finally, on a hot tip from a Moroccan traveler, I took a black trash bag and threw all my possessions into it. I left it out in the hot tropical sun for a week to thoroughly bake and suffocate the little bastards. This, ultimately, was successful.

There are two kinds of travelers in this world.

There's the guy who catches bedbugs and takes care of it.

Then there's the scumbag who, upon picking up a batch of bed bugs, simply moves from hostel to hostel in the hopes that his blood-sucking hitchhikers will move out of his backpack and into another person's belongings. There is a special circle in Hell for the nefarious villains who employ this perfidious practice. (At the very least, they should infinitely reincarnate as bedbugs themselves.)

We just can't have nice things.

Still, I'd rather get bedbugs from a three-dollar hostel in Southeast Asia than from the honeymoon suite at the Hilton. It's a roll of the dice either way, and probably that expensive suite, under black-light examination, is a whole lot filthier.

And no free beer.

25

Still Lost in Translation
まだ翻訳で失われた

At least it's only the one coconut.

SPOTTED IN THAILAND.

I am liten,
my loves...

Spotted in
Korea.

ITCHY FEET TRAVEL TALES 117

Texting and walk is danger.
SPOTTED IN JAPAN.

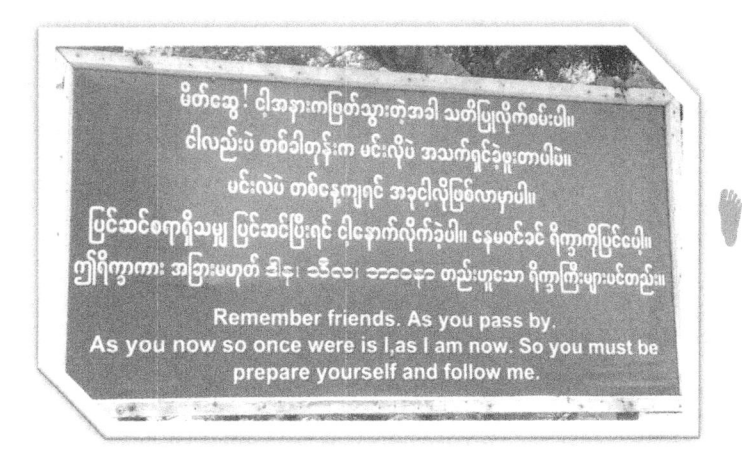

Remember friends. As you pass by.
As you now so once were is I, as I am now. So you must be
prepare yourself and follow me.

I am the walrus. Coo coo kachu.
SPOTTED IN MYANMAR.

26

Local Wildlife: Who Let the Dogs Out
ခွေးသည်ခွေးကိုစားသည်

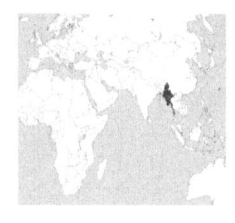

In Mandalay, Myanmar, I had to catch a train. The train I needed only departed once a day, at 4 a.m. The train station was 1 km from my hostel. That's a fifteen-minute walk, so why would I take a cab? Where would I even find a cab at four o'clock in the morning?

Mandalay is a ghost town at night, but even during the day you have to Watch. Your. Step. There are gaping holes all along the sidewalk that plummet twenty feet straight down to the sewer.

I wore my headlamp so I wouldn't fall into the literal underbelly of the city. About every ten paces I was leaping over a crevice that had cracked open.

In Mandalay, man might rule the day, but it's the dogs who rule the night. By day, they mope. By night, they prowl.

No sooner had I rounded the corner from the hostel onto the main road, than a dog emerged from the shadows. A street dog. He threw his head back and howled low and clear. One, two, five, ten feral dogs appeared out of nowhere, heeding the call.

They say it's dumb to run from wild dogs, that they're more likely to give chase. But when you've got a dozen of them pacing and snarling after you, all that advice goes out the window.

There was a car parked on the street about 100 yards ahead. My only hope was to outrun the beasts. I sprinted that football field length with 20 pounds of gear on my back at a speed that would rival a Deion Sanders touchdown return.

I jumped up onto the hatchback just when the pack closed on my heels. They reared up on their hind legs, scratching at the sides of the car and barking their fool heads off. I was trapped.

I heard a door slam from across the street. An old man ran out, waving a broom around his head and shouting at the pack in Burmese. The dogs scattered, retreating back into the shadows.

I climbed down off the car. "That's a good trick," I said, still shaking. "They speak Burmese, huh? What did you tell them?"

"Is not the words," the old man smiled. "You must bark louder than they bark."

27

Spirited Away
адууны сүү

I've had moonshine from Kentucky to Kamchatka; Bosnia to Bali. The best is Siberian Samogon. The worst is Indonesian Arrack.

The highest-selling spirit in the entire world is Korean Soju. You can fact-check me on that. Seeing as it's only the Koreans drinking the stuff, that's impressive. And that's not even taking into account the *Other* Korea's consumption. Who *knows* how much they're drinking north of the DMZ.

Soju is a rice spirit dating back at least 700 years. It's cheap too — about a buck a bottle, or 1,000 Won. All those little dollar-bottles add up to the most liquor sales of any spirit *in the world*.

In Korea, if you are enjoying a single bottle of Soju by yourself, you're an alcoholic. However, if you have food in front of you and you're drinking with even one other person, the two of you can put away a dozen bottles of "happy water" and then you are simply "enjoying your meal." It's a fun game to walk past restaurant fronts in the evening and count the little green bottles that have accrued on the tables. It's a Soju Massacre.

I was teaching at an English Academy in East Seoul. Korean law dictates that schools can't keep the kids past 10 p.m. So we kept them until 9:59. Walking home with fellow teacher and Irish gentleman Keith, we always encountered stumble-drunk Korean men wobbling and weaving across the road, the little green bottles in their hands clung tightly to their chests.

"These people are more bollocksed than back home in Ireland," he commented once, "and that's sayin' something!"

When Korean men "enjoy their meal" a bit *too* much, they just pass out on the sidewalk.

A guy in a suit will be wearing a rolex, have 500,000 Won in his wallet, a brand new Samsung in his pocket, and an iPad folded in his arms — just snoozing away in a drunken stupor right there on the side of the road. Nobody touches him. Nobody dares.

It's an honor culture.

One night, when I was walking home from school, there was a car parked sideways in the middle of the street. I had to shimmy around it. I saw that the driver's door was open and the driver was passed out cold, the top half of his body spilling out supine onto the street with his arms above his head, his legs still inside the car. He had almost made it out. Or in. Nobody bothered him to find out which.

Most Asian spirits are going to be distilled from rice. These are your Japanese Sake, Laotian Lao-Lao, Vietnamese Rượu (tse-ao). The Filipinos use the coconut flower for their Lambanong. The Burmese distill their Htan Yay from palm tree sap.

The Mongolians, as always, are the exception to the rule. They ferment their booze from horse milk.

Really.

The initial distillation produces Airag — a white, rancid yogurt-tasting stuff that has about the same alcohol content as a beer. If you distill it further, and further, and further after that — you'll end up with a truly foul vodka-ish beverage that I cannot recommend even to my worst enemies.

> To learn more about Mongolians and their drinking habits see Chapter 8, *From Breast Milk to Beer — Mongolian Drinking Stories*.

But Indonesian Arrack is the real beast of them all. It is distilled from red rice and sugarcane. Sounds tasty enough, right? Wrong.

Indonesian moonshine is notorious for being poorly manufactured. When you distill liquor improperly, one of the unintended byproducts is methanol. What you're going for in a batch is pure(ish) ethanol.

Ethanol = Dionysian Revelry.

Methanol = Blindness and Death.

When you rush the process, or you don't know what you're doing, you might not successfully distill out the bad stuff.

Like any true moonshine, Indonesian Arrack weighs in at about 70% alcohol per volume. Compare that to your 40% bottle of Jack Daniels. That'll put the hair on your chest *and* burn it off.

If you live to tell the tale.

28

The Rooster and the Egg
Ayam Sabungan dan Telur

I don't know which came first — the Cockfight or the Arrack. But I do know that you can't have one without the other.

I was in Amed, Bali, one of Indonesia's better kept secrets. Located in the Northeast of this paradisiacal little Hindu island in the middle of Islamic Indonesia, Amed is a collection of villages whose roads were only just paved in this century.

The joke is that Bali is the capital of Australia. The Aussies seem to outnumber the locals two to one. But they don't bother with the Northeast portion of the island because the surf is no good (thank God).

One of the major social gatherings among men in Bali is the weekly cockfight. The Balinese call it *tajen*. If I was going to hang out with the locals, that was the place to be. I heard whisperings that it was held on Sundays. Today was Sunday.

Sunday! Sunday! Sunday!

I hopped on my rented motorbike, the tropical sun rising before me. I rode through town, asking everyone I saw, "Where is the *tajen*?" They directed me up into the jungle, along dirt-clod paths. The trail opened up into a large, mown area of grass and dirt where all the village men were gathering, their cocks in their hands.

They were dressed in the traditional batik-patterned kamen — sarong skirts tied off at the waist with a selendang sash belt. On their heads they wore udeng wraps. The udeng topknot made them all look like they had quail plumes, matching the crowns of the proud cocks they carried.

The only white man there, I was dressed in *my* traditional garb of cargo shorts and an Arkansas Razorbacks t-shirt. No hat on my head. No cock in my hand.

I was only there to "observe the local customs" of course. I don't go in for bloodsport.

There was a ring set up in a grove of palm trees, roped off around the trunks. I noticed the only woman there, off to the side, under her own palm tree. She was crouched on a milk crate. Her orange kamen was hiked up to her thighs, and she wore a plain white t-shirt that only served to indicate just how large she was.

She was sitting there, her hands folded in her lap. At her feet was a basket of large brown eggs and a glass gallon jug of brown liquid. "There be the infamous Arrack," I thought.

No one had approached her. I certainly didn't want to be the first to sample the stuff. So I watched. And I waited.

An old man sauntered over. He was not dressed as ornately as the others. He wore a faded blue kamen without a belt, and his white t-shirt matched Our Lady of the Arrack. He had not bothered with an udeng head piece, and his patchy gray hair fell in stringy wisps on the scalp of a head that hung low and hunched to his chest.

He rolled his eyes up and smiled a wide and toothless grin at the madam. They chatted while she produced a glass and poured the brown hooch from the jug. She reached for an egg, cracked it over the edge of the glass and dropped it in the drink.

The old man took it from her with a shaking hand, and thrust out the elbow of his drinking arm to steady himself. He placed his other hand over his forehead with his palm out, leaned back, and tossed the contents right down his toothless gullet. He wiped his mouth and handed her back the glass. He reached in the waistband of his kamen and handed her a wadded Rupiah note. He walked away, this time with a sure step in his stride, shadowboxing the air and pounding his chest.

Well, I guess it's my turn. I strutted over with all the confidence I could muster. She saw me coming. Her eyes widened in surprise, and she smiled with just a few more teeth than the old man.

"Arrack?" I asked, returning the smile.

"Arrack!" she confirmed. Her big, fat hand grabbed a glass from beneath her. Her other hand grasped the jug of fire water. She poured it into the glass. She reached for an egg, cracked it over the side of the glass, and dropped it into my drink.

In imitation of the old man, I stuck out the elbow of my drinking arm, put my other hand to my forehead with palms out, leaned back, and tossed the stuff down my gullet.

GULP.

Sweet Anvil of Hephaestus! Oh frumious Bandersnatch! The flaming bowels of Hades rose up within me to greet the descending demons of a possession most fowl.

I pounded my chest like the old man had done. The fat lady was laughing. She might as well have been singing. 70% my ass. That was straight petrol. With a raw egg in it.

"Calooh Callay!" I choked. I reached into my pocket and handed her a wadded Rupiah note.

While I was thusly pounding my chest, a man ran over to me, the plume of his udeng bobbing with every step. "I am Aman, I speak Englisss!"

"Hey Aman," I croaked, and shoved my hand into his, still wincing from the Arrack.

"You are American-ah?"

"Is it that obvious?"

"Ha!" he laughed. "You have come to for the *tajen*?"

"Sure," I said.

"Come," he took my hand. "I will help to you."

I should take a moment to note that cockfighting in Bali originated as a religious sacrificial ceremony called *Tabuh Rah*. The cocks spill their blood on the ground to ward off evil spirits. Moreover, the owner of each bird projects himself onto his cock — when a man drops his cock into the ring, it becomes a symbolic representation of him. The owner's very reputation is riding on his cock.

All the men had gathered ringside, chatting and counting their money. Aman and I crouched down among them.

The first cock was brought out. Its owner, a tall and handsome fellow, set it on the ground to strut. It was a magnificent bird. Its hackle was a mane of auburn red from its back to its saddle, with breast, wing and tail plumage of a mulberry sheen. Its crown was sharp and crimson. It crowed cool and clear.

The appearance of this specimen excited the crowd. The men shouted and waved their money in the air.

The challenger was introduced. The owner was the old man who had sampled the Arrack before me. His bird looked like a vulture. His neck was sloped down in a curve. He was old, chewed up, and pissed off about it. He may once have been white, but that was many fights and shades of gray ago.

The hackle feathers of his neck were soot-colored and sparse, and here and there patches were plucked out. The sickle feathers of his tail splayed out like a forked tongue. His sickly pink comb hung drooping from his head.

He had one eye, and he seemed to be missing a toe. He paced along the rope, his dipped neck bobbing up and down. But that one eye had the cold, dead look of a killer.

The old man held him by his tail feathers, and the bird emitted a blood-curdling, banshee crow. This was a seasoned gladiator, and he would take no shit.

"Him," I said, pointing to the creature.

"That ugly old man-ah?" cried Aman.

"You betcha," I said, still admiring the bird.

"My friend, that is a bad bet. He has only one eye-ah!"

"What are the odds?"

"Two to one, against."

I pulled a fistful of Rupiah notes out of my pocket. "Bet it all on the old man's cock."

"Okay," he shrugged, and took my money. "You have a place to stay tonight-ah?" inquired Aman.

My backpack was locked up at a hostel down the road, but I hadn't paid for another night. "Yeah, well, I haven't told them yet one way or another."

"My friend," he pointed at a thin man crouched ringside. "He has a very nice bungalow-ah." The thin man looked over and nodded. "He will bet you for one night stay in his bungalow. Very nice."

"A side bet, eh? And if I lose?"

"If you lose, you pay my friend 300,000 Rupiah."

"Twenty bucks?!" I haggled the terms of the bet. "The odds are two-to-one, so tell your man I'll pay him 150,000 if I lose. But if Old Man Chicken wins, then he pays *me* a 150-kicker, *plus* the keys to the bungalow."

Aman turned to his friend and negotiated my parlay. The thin man studied me, and nodded his head.

The cock handler entered the ring, wearing a red udeng head wrap. He tied a pair of curved karembit knives onto each bird's shanks, reinforcing their spurs with razor-sharp talons.

Then the largest man in the village stood and clapped his hands, his belly hanging over his selendang sash. The crowd of men came alive, shouting their bets and waving their money. The big fellow walked around the perimeter of the ring, memorizing everyone's wagers.

The two owners held their cocks by the tail. The hackle feathers bristled on their necks and flared straight out in ruff collars as they pulled and lunged against the tug of their owner's grip.

The handler stood between them with his hand high in the air. He brought it down in a swift chop, and the men released their cocks.

There erupted a clamor of men shouting and howling and waving their fisted money as the birds ran at each other headlong. They reared up in the air and flapped their wings violently, stabbing at each other with their knives. There was a blur and a commotion of feathers.

The fight had been quick and merciful.

The old man's grizzled cock staggered away, limping from the wound in his leg that bled out in thin drops. He raised his bent neck and cawed his banshee crow of victory.

The magnificent red rooster lay lifeless on the ground.

The handler in his red udeng picked up the dead bird, blood matted in its feathers, and dropped it on the ground once, twice, three times, until he was certain that it had ceased to be.

The crowd went wild. The handler grabbed the triumphant cock and removed the knives from his legs, handing him over to his owner, who held him high in the air with a beaming, gummy smile.

Money changed hands. The fat bet-keeper came around and handed my new friend Aman a large wad of Rupiah bills. Aman took them with two hands and dropped the wad into mine.

"Congratulations-ah!"

I had tripled my money. The thin bungalow owner came around behind me with the 150,000 Rupiah in his hand.

"Just buy me a beer," I said, pushing the money away. "And the key to the bungalow, of course."

He smiled sheepishly and spoke to Aman.

"He say he will put the key in the door to the bungalow. I take you to there later."

After the day's festivities, Aman insisted I go with him to meet his family, and then he would show me toced the bungalow.

We rode up the hill to his house. It was a traditional Balinese home, built on a raised stone platform with columns colored in ornate blues and golds, a garden courtyard in the back, and a miniature temple shrine.

I met Mom. And the kids. Even Grandma came out to visit. They were the picture of smiling village life. We sat on the stone patio among the pinwheel frangipani flowers in whites, yellows and pinks. We snacked on disco peanuts and custard milk pies.

"You would like to drink Arrack?" he asked hopefully.

"Never again so long as I live, Aman. How about a nice cold Bintang beer?"

We sipped suds into the sunset as Aman's children played and the women wove batik fabrics on their looms and I waited to go blind from the Arrack I'd had earlier that day.

Maybe it was beginner's luck, but I'm still standing, and my vision is clearer than ever.

I wouldn't necessarily recommend the Arrack, or the cockfight. Unless, of course, you want to travel to the heart of the Balinese people.

29

Everybody Poops
私の好きなトイレ

When ya gotta go, ya gotta go. Because shit happens. And when you're eating new and interesting foods on a sojourn in Asia, it can happen at the drop of a conical bamboo hat.

Knowing how and where to do Number Two in a foreign country is crucial, or else you'll be kissing your favorite pair of panties goodbye.

Public defecation is always an option.

Park Pooper

Parks are a popular place to pop a squat. I've even seen a Chinese man drop trow right in the middle of the median of a busy multi-lane Beijing thoroughfare. And I've seen grown men laying turds on the tracks all along the rail to Rishikesh.

If you prefer to make your confession in a private booth, it never hurts to ask for directions.

A note for Americans: we're the only ones who call it a "bathroom."

Not if, but when you find yourself doing the bubble-gut shuffle, the word "toilet" is pretty universal. And if the locals stare back blankly as you desperately shout *TOILET!* louder and louder, you can always resort to miming (with the addition of some elementary school sound effects).

No matter where you are in Asia, you're bound to find a squat potty on every corner. These holes in the ground are not just relegated to third-world countries. Even Samsung executives hunch on their haunches at the public privy. (Doctors actually agree that this is the most ergonomic position for successful evacuations. Just remember to shift your center of gravity forward and clear the landing strip. You don't want to fall in or otherwise get any on ya.)

Some people evidently love squatting it out so much that, even when presented with Western-style facilities, they still prefer to climb on top of the commode and hover precariously over the bowl like they're poised to swan-dive into a swimming pool. I know this because I have seen shoe prints (and digested curry) on toilet seats.

This practice is shunned in "proper" Asian bathrooms. There are cautionary signs posted in every flush-tank lavatory depicting a stick man standing on top of the toilet seat. The big red circle with the line slashed through is stamped on top of our delinquent friend.

If you've got the grumpy dumpies in Southeast Asia, the facilities may *appear* Western in style. But at the critical moment, look around for the toilet paper dispenser, and it's not there. In its place is a water hose with a pistol grip nozzle. This is referred to affectionately as the "bum gun" and I'll take it over the rough stuff any day.

Always, *always* test the water pressure first. If you're not careful, some of these trigger-hair geysers will give you a colonic until water shoots out of your nose.

The Japanese are crackerjack at perfecting the quality of everything under the sun, and they didn't stop at Number Two. Even their McDonald's bathroom stalls have seats that are equipped with motorized, push-button bidets.

There's a blue button with a diagram of a man squeezing one out. Pushing this button brings the bidet whirring to life from inside the bowl beneath you. Pucker up, because a jet of water is about to shoot right up into your bullseye like a classic carnival game. (Ladies, there's a pink button for you. Take it for a spin.)

My favorite button on the armrest panel is a music note icon. Press it down, and it plays a little tune to drown out the sound of your farts. Very... courteous.

So everybody poops. Same-Same, but different.

And if you're afraid of dropping the kids off at the pool with no towels, stuff some 2-ply in your back pocket.

30

Pics or It Didn't Happen
ไม่จำเป็นต้องใช้รูปถ่าย

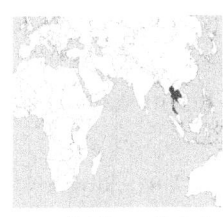

Sometimes you forget to take the picture. Or ten. Or twenty — and a video. You kick yourself later, after the moment has passed and its sublimity sinks in:

"Why didn't I bust out the phone and push a button?"

"It would've been so easy to document this."

"Dammit, this will never happen again, and now it's lost forever..."

But it is precisely in these moments — these most real and human moments — that we happily forget our Facebook-generation, documentarian obligations.

And we actually enjoy life, instead of becoming another tourist in a sea of selfie-sticks.

So it was one day at Wat Arun Temple in Bangkok, Thailand. After a week of heavy adventuring and even heavier shutter-clicking about this gorgeous country, I had such a moment.

I boarded the overcrowded ferry to cross the Chao Praya River, the main watery artery of Bangkok. With a whistle from the conductor we were off, chuggling along what is effectively an open sewer, to the other side. Forced against the handrail, I took care to keep my mouth closed, lest a droplet of water splash up into my face and set any variety of nasty parasites going to work on my immune system.

My day of temple-hopping had led me from the Grand Palace down to Wat Pho and the giant reclining Buddha. Last on the list was the Temple of Dawn, Wat Arun, its main spire rising above the thin smog.

The ferry docked with a jolt and I brushed through the crowd.

I wish I could tell you how ethereal the Temple of Dawn appeared before me in its quintessential Khmer architecture, how I ascended the three symbolic levels of enlightenment inherent in its design until I reached the Trident of Shiva, how I looked out across the river at Old Town Bangkok and its gilded temples for that requisite photo-op.

I wish I could tell you all of that, and have the picture to prove it.

But sometimes, when you go to look at what the past has preserved, it's in the act of being preserved. You can't have it both ways. When I visited the Coliseum in Rome, it was half-covered in scaffolding. A good number of cathedrals across Europe, too. Sometimes you get lucky, sometimes you don't. I wasn't lucky with Wat Arun.

So there goes the photo, I thought. The Temple of Dawn was roped off, its base enshrouded in pipe and drape.

I climbed up the stony steps, past inlaid statues of Hindu gods, until coming up against yellow tape wrapped around the whole of the edifice there. I walked around either side, hoping to find some passage upwards but was greeted only by more tape. Crudely improvised red and yellow twine had been strung across the steps, tied from the outcropping of a demon's finger to a stony elephant tusk, anchored by gallon water jugs.

I was stuck at the base level of Wat Arun's *Traiphum* — that level signifying this realm of existence. There was no way I could achieve the highest level of *Devaphum* — the "heavenly realm of happiness." I couldn't even move upwards to *Tavatimsa* — the level of "contentment where all desires are gratified." Unless of course, I was willing to risk the wrath of the temple guards and thusly the Thai Police, with whom I'd already had not-so-pleasant dealings.

So I took what pictures I could. The most visible figure through the tape and the drape was a relief carving of the Kinnari. The Kinnari — half goddess, half swan, with her Khmer pointed crown, dancing in a folded-hand pose. I've seen her all over Thailand, even in subway terminals.

So I climbed down. Down from the enlightenment that was withheld from me. Dejected, I circled the base of the monument.

I smelled food.

In a corner of the temple grounds, people were gathered around a buffet table, spread out with all assortment of traditional Thai dishes. A woman noticed me. She smiled.

"Sawat dee krab," I said, respectfully pressing my palms together and bowing to her.

"Sawat dee krab," she replied. "You like some food?"

"Sure," I said, eyeing the smorgasbord. "How much?"

"Is not for sell," she cackled. "This our family."

I had crashed a family reunion. These were uncles and aunts, cousins, grandmothers and babies. Looking around, I guessed there were at least four generations represented.

My sunburned face flushed even redder. "Oh. Oh no. I'm so sorry. I didn't realize…"

"Please," she said. "We fill our plates, and now we make offering. Please, join our family."

I had interrupted something sacred. As though I had barged in on a family's Christmas dinner in the middle of Dad carving the turkey. I was uninvited, and yet, welcomed.

I was there. I was hungry. I was humble. And that was good enough for them.

"You call me Ba."

"Thank you, Ba. You call me Sam."

"Sam…" She sat me down in a plastic chair next to a young woman. "That is Pensri." She motioned toward the girl. "She have good English."

Pensri pressed her palms together in greeting. Her arms were long and elegant, even statuesque. Almost, indeed, like the Kinnari. "Sawat dee krab." A smile stretched across her face, up to her high cheek bones, her parting and pouty lips revealing big white teeth.

"Sawat dee krab," I replied. "Pensri is a lovely name."

Ba and the other women all laughed to each other.

Ba addressed the entire family in her shrill Thai. A chorus of "Sawat dee Krab" rang out around the long table.

Ba brought me dish after dish, insisting that I "must try one and one and all of food." There was Gai Thod — Thai fried chicken, crispy and juicy on a bed of long rice. Ladle scoops of Christmas-colored curries were heaped on top, swimming in coconut milk with peppers and pork, topped with peanuts. There was Pla Boo — whole fish, poached and garlic-citrusy. Everyone dug their fingers into its side for pinches of meat. You weren't going to find this at the street food stalls. This was down-home cookin'.

It wasn't out of politeness that I licked every plate clean. It's that it was all so damn good.

"These are our ancestors' favorite foods," said Pensri. "We are gathered here at the temple today to honor them."

"Your ancestors have good taste," I said as dessert came rolling out. There was Sangkhaya — a squash custard. Khao Niao Sangkhaya — sticky rice with coconut custard. And a squid egg custard I had never seen before nor probably will again. They were all delicious in a wholesome way that decadent western sweets can't touch.

Pensri laughed, an honest, gentle laugh. "I hope you have enjoyed our Thai people and culture."

"Yes, indeed. You have a lovely family," I said. "Thank you for... everything."

She pressed her palms together in farewell with those slender Kinnari arms. "I hope you come back soon."

"I hope so too."

I stood to make my exit as modestly as possible, but Ba ran over to me, her brow furrowed, and grasped me by the arm.

"You no can go now," she pleaded.

"But Ba, I've had a one and one and all, of everything," I said. "Thank you!"

"You must have two and two of all!" She insisted.

"And three and four?" I teased.

She cackled in laughter and threw her sure, mothering arms around me. I embraced her back.

"Goodbye!" I shouted to everyone. "Thank you so much!" We all erupted in a round of "Sawat dee krabs" and I took off, back toward the temple, for the river.

Pensri smiled enigmatically and waved until I disappeared around the corner.

I looked up at Wat Arun for the last time. Cloaked in its billowing veil, the setting sun glinting off the top Trident of Shiva. In all my frustration of not being able to climb up it, up to the topmost layer of the Devaphum realm of happiness, I realized that I actually had. It had come over me without my knowing it, what the Buddhists call *Satipaṭṭhāna*, or "mindfulness of the now."

I had no picture of Pensri and her family. Only a fullness in my belly and a fullness in my heart.

No photograph could capture that.

To have taken out the camera would have been to taint the memory, for however long it lasts. It's the butterfly you could've caught with your net and taken home to your collection of other insects, pinned all in a row behind glass. But instead, you let that one get away, watching it flutter into the sun to live out its days.

And you'll never forget it.

Because it touched you.

31

In an Octopus's Garden
링고가이 노래를 부른다

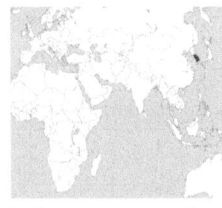

It was New Year's Eve, and some friends and I decided we would experience a new (to us) Korean delicacy: Live Octopus. As in, an octopus which is alive. And you put it in your mouth, and you eat it.

We met at the Noryangjin Fish Market in Seoul, a massive warehouse with an open ground floor of soaking wet concrete pathways. We navigated the damp matrix, past aquariums of red fish, blue fish, live fish, dead fish.

There's a salmon section, a squid section, one for tuna and one for yellowtail, shark and shrimp. There are also baffling and surreal creatures of the deep whose existence I had never before fathomed. And apparently people eat them.

We strolled through the stinking place, touring the cast of "Finding Nemo" and dodging motorbikes that drive right down the aisles making deliveries of fresh catches from the Yellow Sea coast.

There they were — whatever the plural of "octopus" is. Octopi? Octopodes? No one can agree.

Anyway, there they were — live octopus-eses swimming in a tank. These were the dwarf variety, small enough to fit perfectly on a dinner plate.

We haggled with the lady fish monger in the best Korean we could muster. It's always good to learn the numbers in the local language because, after standing our ground, we saved about $3 US on our octopus. That was enough for a few road beers after our barbaric meal.

She stuck her hand into the tank and grabbed our boy, popping his suction cupped tentacles away from the glass.

The urge came upon me to call it off, to take our octopus home and keep him as a pet in the bathtub. But we were already in too deep.

The upstairs of the Noryangjin wet market is lined with small restaurants. The idea is to pick out your aquatic lunch and take it into one of these kitchens where the cook prepares it to your liking.

You've heard of "farm to table?" This is "sea to chopstick."

We marched up the stairs, following our fish lady who carried our octopus in a mesh net. He was sending his eight tentacles out in every direction, trying to pull himself up over the lip of the net. She kept prying him off the sides and shoving him back to the bottom of the mesh.

We kicked our shoes off at the first restaurant entrance and were seated at a low table. Our server set up individual ramekins of red gochujang pepper dipping sauces and exited with a bow. She re-emerged from the kitchen with our wriggling blue friend on a plate. We stared at him in silence for some time, long enough for him to maneuver his way out of the serving dish and slink onto the wooden table.

She produced a butcher knife and pointed it at me. I shook my head no. She laughed and nodded yes. She brought the knife down on the table with a *thwack*, amputating a tentacle from the body.

She grabbed a pair of metal chopsticks and picked up the spasming tentacle. "Okay," she said, handing it to me.

The tentacle was wrapping itself around my chopstick. Live octopus is probably the number one choking hazard in the world. The tentacle will crawl and writhe and attempt to attach itself to whatever it can. Which, in this case, is your throat. Those suction cups will clasp on and not let go, blocking your windpipe and asphyxiating you. Your only hope then would be for someone to shove their hand down your larynx and try to pop the suction cups loose.

I dipped it into my sauce. I put my teeth over the chopstick and scraped the thing off. It squirmed inside my mouth.

"Chew!" my buddy yelled.

I bit down hard and didn't stop. I must've chewed for a solid two minutes. It tasted like fresh octopus alright. Sentient saltwater jerky. Not my favorite. I chased it down my throat with a swig of soju rice wine and gulped. The octopus had not won today.

The rest of my friends followed in suit until the poor deformed thing was a four-legged quadropus. It was twisting and flailing, still fighting for life.

"Put the bloody thing out of its misery!" I cried, motioning to our server to kill it dead. She chopped off its head, its tentacles still seeking escape.

I jumped up. "I gotta go find a bag of chips and a coke, or whatever is the opposite of *this*."

"You want us to save you the leftovers?" my buddy teased, the table erupting in laughter. I slipped my shoes back on and walked out of the market.

Happy freakin' New Year.

32

Chopsticks: Whatever Wok's
空中からハエを奪う

To remember how to conduct oneself at a nice Japanese restaurant, I've composed a useful nursery rhyme:

One, Two - Take off shoes
Three, Four - Sit on the floor
Five, Six - Use chopsticks
Seven, Eight - Keep them straight

I never learned how to "properly" use chopsticks. One through Six aren't a problem. But Seven, Eight? I don't "keep them straight."

I cross my chopsticks. This is not impolite or "bad form" so much as it elicits curious stares and snickers from other diners.

Imagine eating pudding with a person who holds the spoon backwards in her clenched fist. Or a grown man clutching a pencil like a kindergartner colors with a crayon.

That is literally how Asian people describe my chopstick method.

I prefer to think of myself as a pitcher with a goofy underhand who nevertheless delivers the baseball over home plate every time.

I've been living in Asia for five years, and I still stick out. Waiters and kitchen ladies all over the continent notice my awkward technique — the sticks at an almost perpendicular angle in my hand — and they bring me a fork. I always refuse the patronizing gesture and demonstrate plucking a single grain of rice successfully in my pincers. "Ta-Da!" I'll say, as they stare in bewilderment.

They still laugh at me, of course. But I challenge anyone to a chopstick speed-eating contest.

CHOPSTICK ETIQUETTE
DON'T:
- Park chopsticks upright in your food.
- Point at people with chopsticks.
- Stab food with chopstick.
- Stab people with chopstick.
- Pass food with chopsticks.
- Suck on chopsticks.
- Clean earwax with chopstick.
- Swashbuckle with chopstick.
- Play drums with chopsticks.
- Stick chopsticks up nostrils.

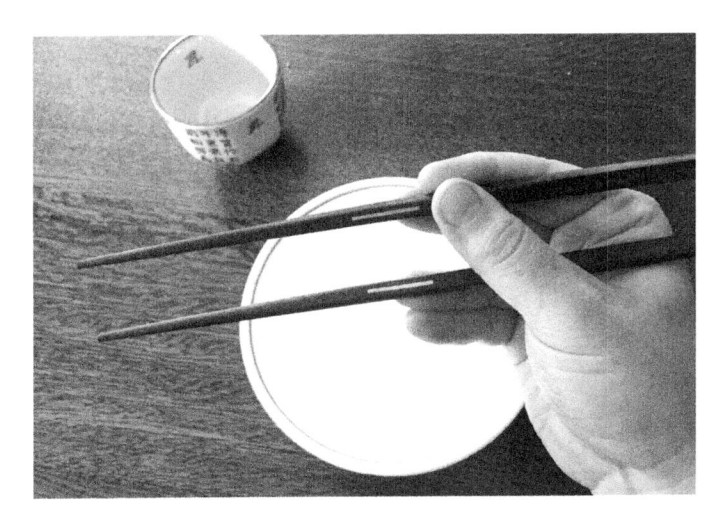

The Correct Way — Rest the bottom chopstick in the groove of your thumb and steady it with your ring finger. Hold the top stick between your thumb and first two fingers.

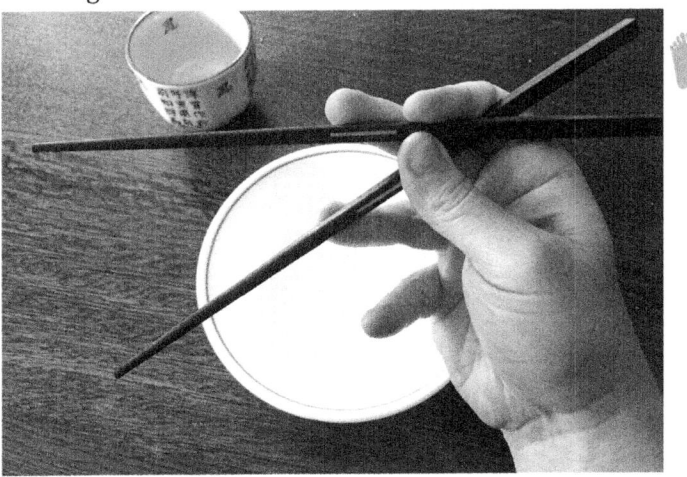

My Way — Whatever this is. I don't really know. But it does make for an interesting shadow puppet.

Those Who Don't Shout Don't Eat
봉사하고 있습니다.

Yelling for a waiter might seem in bad form according to your western sense of etiquette. I assure you it is not. Otherwise, you won't get served. In fact, each Asian culture has its own unique way of summoning staff.

In North America, not only is it rude to wave a waitress down, but she will bother you at the worst possible moments — when you're in mid-conversation, when you've just taken a bite of your burger, when you're proposing to your girlfriend. And then you have to tip them 20% of the bill!

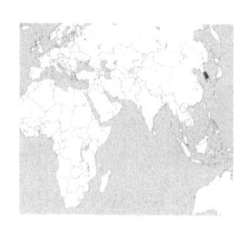

Enter a Korean restaurant and shout, "Jeogiyo!" (Or, "give me service.") You'll hear a chorus of "Neeeh!" from the kitchen. That's a resounding "Yeeesss" and a confirmation that you're ready to order.

In Vietnam, it's slightly more complicated. Addressing anyone is both gender and age-based. There are uncles, aunties, and people your age or younger — Ang's, Chi's, and Em's, respectively. For example, if it's a woman older than yourself, ring out a "Chi" followed with a fun "Oi!" and they'll come over. Well, maybe after your third or fourth attempt.

Myanmar's the most fun. To get a waiter's attention, make a loud kissy sound. A packed cafe at lunchtime is a symphony of smooches. This takes considerable practice to be louder than the roar of conversation and canoodles. But never fail, if you can kiss the air with the best of them, a waiter shall appear.

Here's a tip: Don't.
"Tipping" is not a city in China. Or anywhere else in Asia, for that matter. Over here, a tip is not expected. You pay for what you eat. No more, no less.

Call for service at this establishment, and they don't bring toilet paper, but fried chicken. This is *Chicken Toilet* in Seoul, Korea. It's a latrine-themed restaurant that actually serves up some decent wings.

34

Ruined Restaurants and Hidden Gems
Bún chả ngon là một bí mật

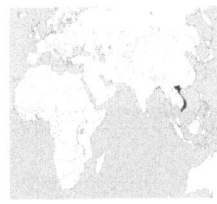

The best way to ruin a restaurant is to recommend it. Any establishment that gets a Tripadvisor or Lonely Planet shout-out quickly goes from humble to huddled.

The Hanoi restaurant where Anthony Bourdain treated President Obama to bún chả might as well be a museum now. The two men toasted bottles of Bia Hanoi and shot the breeze over noodles and flame-broiled pork belly as the cameras rolled in this simple snack shack. Today, if you go to Bún Chả Hương Liên (better known now as Bun Cha Obama), you'll fight a line that wraps around the block.

And now there's even less seating space inside Bún Chả Hương Liên. They've taken that middle table where Obama sat on his first visit to Vietnam and encased it in glass. What used to be a local secret is now a tourist destination.

So I'm hesitant to mention specific restaurants that get my love. I'll just say, as a rule: follow the local crowd. Eschew the tourist traps. If there's a bunch of old white people with cameras around their necks waiting in line for a bowl of Japanese ramen, keep walking. If there's an English menu on a sandwich board, pass it by.

```
Here's a tip: If you're ever at a loss
for what to order, meander about the
dining hall and have a look at what
everybody's eating. When you see
something that looks good, call the
wait staff over and point at that dish.
```

Eating at the best dives can be a worthwhile, but challenging experience. Not only is the menu in the local language, but you also have to order *in* that language.

As far as Vietnam goes — get lost. When you walk around any square block in Hanoi, you'll unwittingly pass at least a dozen kitchens of true and ancient flavor that are nestled deep in the neighborhood corners. Why not wander down winding backstreets until you smell what the locals are cookin'?

A bowl of mỳ vằn thắn just tastes better on a plastic stool.

When I take friends out to a favorite bún chả spot in Hanoi, they stroll right past it every time. We double back and enter an anonymous alley that opens up into a packed crowd of hungry Hanoians hunched over plastic stools and slurping up the good stuff.

This buried treasure hunt will never cease to inspire me. It's a never-ending quest — to seek out those hidden culinary gems, shielded against time and tourists' touch.

Bún chả at one of my favorite Hanoi spots.

35

Easy on the Soy Sauce, Old Man
お父さんが恋しい

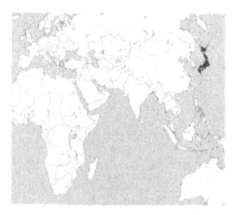

My dad spent his high school years in Japan. He also grew up in such exotic locales as Michigan and Texas, but he got to be a teenager in the Land of the Rising Sun.

He was an "Air Force brat." His dad was an Air Force chaplain. The U.S. military moved Lt. Col. Letchworth's family around, from country to country in the highly strategic procedure whereby a general pulls a name out of a hat and throws a dart at a world map. (I suspect this is the same protocol employed when deciding what country the United States should invade next.)

Dad never much went in for Japanese cuisine. Well, other than always drenching his rice in a pint of soy sauce until every white grain turned black. He was fifty-five the first time he tried sushi. At a Chinese buffet. In Arkansas. Probably he thought that *sashimi* was a dance move from the 1920s.

In fact, growing up, my family never dined on international cuisine (what we still called "ethnic food" in the 90s). No Thai noodles. No Indian curries. Certainly nothing with fish unless it was the whiskered breaded-and-fried variety dipped in tartar sauce. My parents' idea of international food was pizza delivery on Friday nights. Buon appetito.

During his time in Japan, I don't know how often Dad got "into the economy," which is military jargon for "the real world outside the base." I imagine many of his meals consisted of bologna and white bread procured from the Air Force canteen.

He would, however, go on and on about this one Japanese dish. "Katsudon," he'd say with a smile of nostalgia. "Our maid in Japan would always make me katsudon."

I travelled to Osaka a few years ago, the food capital of Japan. It also seems to be the only city in the entire country that stays open past 10 pm. I got in late and headed straight for the lively Dotonbori District. I strolled past a dizzying array of flashing neon lights and restaurants, when I saw a sign in the window of a little ramen shop advertising "Katsudon."

Almost all restaurant transactions in Japan are done through a machine. I dropped a fistful of Yen coins into the coin slot, and pushed the button marked "Katsudon." The machine spit out a ticket with a number on it (Domo Arigato, Mr. Roboto).

I plopped down on a stool at the wooden counter, taking in the symphony of slurping all around me. This was exciting — I couldn't wait to call my father and share a little father/son culinary bonding experience, which up to now had maybe only happened over hot dogs and hamburgers.

I tore my wooden chopsticks out of their paper sleeve, separating them with that satisfying *snap* that commences my mouth to salivating like Pavlov's dog to the dinner bell.

The chef slid a plate in my direction. It was a breaded, pan-fried pork cutlet over rice.

"Katsudon?" I asked.

"Katsudon," said the chef.

Otherwise known as schnitzel, katsudon was imported from the German world to Japan in the 1900s. Turns out that my dad's favorite "Japanese dish" is from Vienna, Austria.

But, as with most things, the Japanese do it better.

A year later, my father got called up to the big schnitzel in the sky. I still set my rice a'swimming in soy sauce in his memory.

Dad in front of an Italian restaurant — pretty much the extent of his culinary adventures.

36

A Whiter Shade of Pale
Phụ nữ da màu đẹp

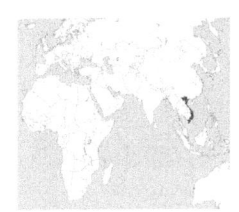

Fair skin is a standard of beauty in many East Asian cultures. It seems to be a status symbol — the darker your skin, the more time you've spent working in the fields. The lighter your skin, the more time you've spent, I dunno... never leaving the house? A bit, hmmm... medieval if you ask me.

In Vietnam, it is a sign of economic prestige for men to grow their fingernails to a Guinness Book of Records length. This is to indicate that they count money for a living (as opposed to picking up hammers and sickles I suppose).

Vietnamese women take the preservation of their skin tone to a level of discomfort. When you see them riding their motorbikes on the street, they are completely covered from head to toe. Especially on blisteringly hot summer days when the sun is shining brightly. There are special riding jackets for women that zip all the way up to the chin, with little mittens sewn onto the ends of the sleeves to keep the sun off their hands. A face mask and Jackie-O sunglasses complete the ensemble. Someone would make a pretty penny selling burqas to these ladies of Hanoi.

When I first moved to Vietnam, I went shopping for toiletries at the local VinMart. I had a list:
- Soap
- Deodorant
- Toilet Paper

Straight away, I couldn't find the toilet paper. I guess I really was meant to be using that water hose next to the commode and soaking my pants every time I take a crap.

There was only one brand of deodorant. Really? Everyone in Vietnam smells exactly the same? That has got to be the single most communist thing I've ever seen. Why, that's more communist than the bloody redistribution of wealth!

I inspected the soap aisle. Every single bar and bottle and body wash contained *whitening agent*. Trust me, I checked.

So I'm going to smell like a communist, I won't be wiping my butthole with toilet paper, but I WILL be bleaching it with whitening soap. Got it.

Lookit, if I get any whiter, I'm going to look like Nasferatu. I'm already only a shade off from albino. Darkening soap, if you got it, please.

Here's what these Asian ladies don't understand — we men don't care about your skin tone. In fact, I personally prefer darker women. Give me a Caramel Cutie, a Sycamore Sweetie, or a Mocha Mama over a Pale Polly any day.

And for the love of Ho Chi Minh, stop riding around on motorbikes dressed up like ninjas.

37
#TeachingInNam
Học chăm chỉ

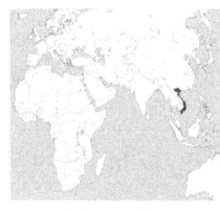

I've been teaching Asian kids how to speak the good English since 2015. I spent eighteen months in Korea, teaching at a private English Academy. The average class size was 10 students.

In Vietnam, where I spent the bulk of my time, I taught in public high schools with 50 kids per class.

This experience has been good, challenging fun.

Mostly.

Maybe you've seen that Nazi rally where Hitler just stands there, combing his hair with his hand and waiting patiently for everyone in the hall to shut the hell up before he starts speaking.

That's me in a classroom of 50 Vietnamese high school students.

Hitler had better luck.

#AnimalSounds

It's always fun to ask kids what sounds the animals make in their language.

For example, the Vietnamese cow goes *Um Bo* not *Moo*.

The Vietnamese chicken goes *Cuc Ta* not *Cluck, Cluck*.

The Vietnamese dog goes *Quau, quau* not *Woof, Woof* (That is, before it goes *THUD* on the dinner plate).

I asked a student what sound the pig makes in Vietnam.

Nguyen blurted out, "All Capitalist Pigs speak English!"

Touché young Nguyen. Touché.

#DairyDisappointment

"Ok class, who can give me an example of *disappointment*? Yes, Hoang?"

"Cheese."

"Why is cheese a disappointment, Hoang?"

"Because when I try cheese, it look like dessert, it feel like dessert, but when I eat the cheese it is sour, not sweet."

Well, *my* example of 'disappointment' is your opinion about cheese, Hoang.

#FamilyNames

The day's lesson was on family member names — daughter, uncle, step-mother, etc. I asked the high school class, "What is the name for your previous wife?"

Quan stood up from the back of the room.

"Bitch?"

Yes and no, Quan. But extra points for pronunciation.

#WordsBeginningWith

Me: Ok students, what's a good multi-syllable word that begins with the letter Y?

(I notice Minh is reading and not paying attention.)

How about you, Minh?

Minh: Yggdrasil.

Me: ...I'm sorry — an *yggdrasil*?

Minh: An yggdrasil is a massive, mythological tree that connects the nine worlds in Norse cosmology.

Me: ...Yeah... I was looking for something more like 'Yesterday'...but that works...

Minh goes back to reading his book as I google *yggdrasil*.

#TheMummyLives

I'm explaining the difference between British vs. American spelling.

"Brits spell *colour* with a *u*, but in America we drop the *u*. Same as in *neighbour* and *favourite*. Can anyone think of another word that differs from American English where the British spelling uses a *u*?"

A hand goes up.

I call on Anh.

"Mum?"

Yes Anh, I'll count it. Americans don't go around sounding like cockney caricatures. Indeed, we rightly dropped the *u* on *Mom*.

#FoneClub

Ladies and gentlemen. Welcome to Mr. Sam's Class.

The First Rule of Mr. Sam's Class is: You do not use your phone in Mr. Sam's Class.

The Second Rule of Mr. Sam's Class is: You do not. Use. Your phone. In Mr. Sam's Class.

If you break the first two rules of Mr. Sam's Class — You HAVE to give Mr. Sam your phone.

I don't know what it is about these kids. They think they're being oh so sly, that from my vantage point at the front of the class, I couldn't possibly see that they're staring down at the phone in their lap, absorbed in a game or a text conversation. Even if there are 50 of them to surveil at once.

They're so hypnotized by the screen that they don't see me strutting slowly down the aisle towards them until their buddy nudges them at the last minute, and they pop back upright to rejoin reality, slipping the phone into their desk with an audible *clunk*.

"Hand it over," I say. "The game is up. Literally."

They always pretend that they have no earthly idea what I'm talking about. "Teacher... what?" they protest, showing me their empty hands.

"I see you on your phone," I tell them. "Everybody sees you on your phone." I point to the portrait above the chalkboard. "Even Ho Chi Minh sees you on your phone." And I stand there with my hand outstretched for as long as it takes them to finally give it up.

My personal record for confiscated phones in a class period is 7. Next semester I hope to double that record.

#HangingWithTheGuards

One day in Hanoi, I showed up for my high school class only to discover that school got canceled at the last minute. No money today.

The school guards were still hanging out in their little guard shack by the front gate. They were drinking beer and eating fried chicken. Those were two words in Vietnamese that I actually knew. We chugged bia and gorged on gà rán all afternoon, until we all needed a taxi or wife to come pick us up.

The next day's English lesson would be on the virtues of not drinking your weight in beer with Vietnamese men. Please turn off the overhead lights and write your essays quietly.

#UncleHoIsAlwaysWatching

Every public classroom in Vietnam has a framed picture of Ho Chi Minh, the great liberator, hanging above the chalkboard.

Ho Chi Minh is everywhere. He even watches all activities inside and outside of the school's third floor stairwell.

It's one of those portraits where his eyes follow you around the room. Like Mona Lisa, but with a kind, grandfatherly smile and a wispy chin-beard. It's eerily comforting.

One day I walked into my high school class and looked up above the chalkboard. Ho Chi Minh was gone!

"What have you done with Uncle Ho?!" I asked the class. "Where is he?"

"He live in our heart, teacher," said one boy, without a hint of sarcasm.

I still sent a student to the office to print out a color copy of Ho Chi Minh's visage, and helped him stand on a desk and tape it above the chalkboard. It just didn't seem right to start class without Uncle Ho watching on, smiling down like Communist Jesus on all us poor sinners.

#YouLoveMeYouReallyLoveMe

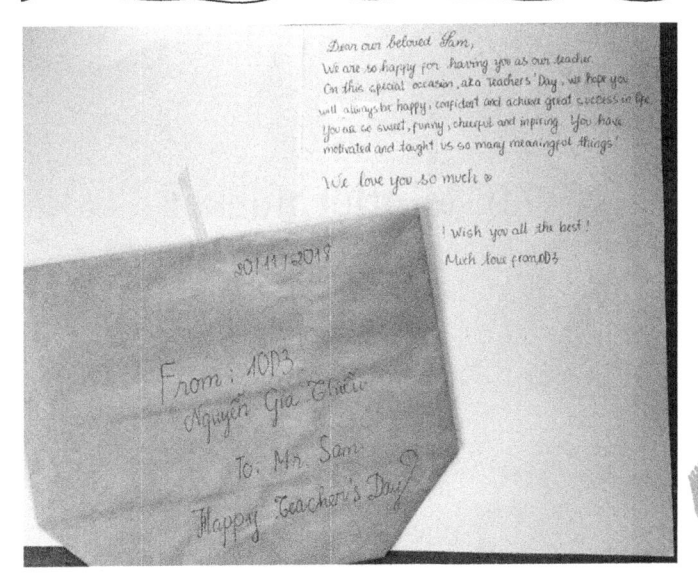

November 20 is Teacher's Day in Vietnam. Students and parents that wish to show appreciation do so in the form of letters and flowers. All the feels.

38

Mr. Mufflerplucker
Không còn chàng trai tốt

It was the first day of school. I walked into the Senior High classroom with my teaching assistant. The 50 students rose to their feet and, in Vietnamese classroom protocol, shouted in unison, "Good Morning Teacher!"

Vietnamese people are typically short in stature, but a big boy in the last row towered above the class. I'm 5 foot 10 and this 17-year-old had a good five inches on me.

"Good Morning Students!" I replied, and they returned to their seats. I introduced myself as Mr. Sam, and wrote my name on the chalkboard.

"Mr. Mufflerplucker," said the Young Buffalo in the last row with a wide grin.

Except he didn't say "Mufflerplucker."

"Get out," I said matter-of-factly, and pointed to the door. He laughed and shook his head.

I looked to my teaching assistant for some, well, assistance. After all, her job was to act as disciplinarian so I would be free to teach. She simply shrugged.

She would later tell me that she thought I should have hit the boy. The 17-year-old boy. "He would never, never dare say that to a Vietnamese teacher. He knows he would go home bloody, or worse."

It should be noted that the educational environment in Vietnam is "Old School."

The fence was being tested and if I let it go I knew that I would be overrun for the rest of the semester.

I walked down the aisle, past rows of giggling students, and stopped at his desk. He barely fit inside of it, his long giraffe legs overflowing into the row in front of him.

"You're out," I told him, gesturing like a baseball umpire.

He just kept beaming, quite proud of himself. The rest of the class was still laughing nervously, wide-eyed, waiting to see what would happen next.

What happened next is that I grabbed him by the scruff of his school uniform collar and pulled him up, right out of his seat. I marched him down the aisle to the door, kicked it open, and threw him outside, slamming the door behind me.

"Right," I said, dusting off my hands. "Where were we? Ah yes. My name is Mr. Sam." I pointed at the board. "Let's all say it together."

"Mr. Sam," said 49 students in perfect unison.

The introductory lesson continued with some fun getting-to-know-you games. The class was uncharacteristically attentive and well-behaved.

After about ten minutes, the boy rapped lightly on the door. I gave the class a quick assignment to write a short introduction about themselves. I opened the door. The young man's head was held low. Still, he had a few inches on me.

"Yes?"

"I so sorry, Teacher," he said, not making eye contact.

"Do you know what respect means?"

"Yes, Teacher."

"Are you going to show respect in my class?"

"Yes, Teacher," he mumbled, his head still hung low, shuffling his shoes.

"What's your name?"

He raised his eyes to meet mine. "Lap."

"What's *my* name?"

He paused. "Mr. Sam?"

"Ok, Lap. Come back and join the class."

For the entire semester that I taught at that high school, Lap would greet me at the gates of the school each day with a broad smile. "Hello Mr. Sam!" he would beam, and insist on carrying my things. He participated eagerly in class, and became one of my best students.

No one's called me Mr. Mufflerplucker since. But if they want him, they'll get him.

39

Slaughter in the School Zone
Bán thịt nguội tươi

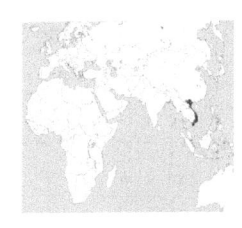

I was teaching at a public high school in the Old Quarter of Hanoi's Hoan Kiem Lake district. This is a very popular area with lots of foot traffic. I walked across the courtyard towards the school gates to have my 10-minute cigarette break between classes. I put the cigarette in my mouth, lighter in hand. I heard the most awful, blood-curdling screams. It took me a moment to identify the sound as coming from a pig. What were they doing to that pig?

I walked outside the school gate. Right there, on the sidewalk in front of the school, three men were hog-tying a giant sow that was squealing for its life.

The high-pitched cries were deafening. Two of the men sat on top of it, and the third man took a very large knife and stuck it in the animal's jugular. He twisted the blade. The screaming stopped. The pig spasmed and then became still. Blood came flowing from the wound.

The men crouched before the sacrifice with ceramic bowls, filling them from the geyser of blood. They raised their bowls in a toast and took a drink.

Then they swaddled the sow in a baby-blue tarp, and hoisted the carcass, with some difficulty, onto the back of a motorbike. They strapped it down, and one of the men jumped on and drove away with it. The other two men spread some leaves over the bloody spot on the sidewalk and set them on fire to burn off the blood. Then they picked up their blood bowls and walked away down the road.

The bell rang, and I had to get back to class. I didn't even get to light my cigarette.

ITCHY FEET TRAVEL TALES 177

> This is the gate of the school campus.

40

Racial Slurs in Context
Chúc mừng Giáng sinh, chiến tranh là hoàn thành

In addition to my day job in Vietnam's public schools, I also taught groups of students in private homes. I'd been teaching a group of five boys every Wednesday. These eighth graders were scary smart, with English reading levels higher than most of my graduating high school class. I always looked forward to Wednesdays.

After two years, they'd become comfortable with me and had developed a penchant for distracting me with queries about American slang and curse words.

Boys will be boys.

"Teacher, what's a douchebag?" they asked me, snickering under their breath.

"I don't know," I lied. "Look it up."

That was a mistake. One boy grabbed the Learner's Dictionary off the table and found the definition, reading it aloud for the class. They fell out of their chairs in hysterics.

"Now you see why that's not a nice thing to call your friend," I scolded them.

The following week, they had a new topic for me. This one came from the top student of the five, Henry.

"Teacher, did the soldiers have slang names for Vietnamese in The American War?" [1]

"Yes Henry, they surely did. Those names are called 'racial epithets' and they're very offensive." I wrote the word "epithet" on the board.

"Do you know the epithets, Teacher? We cannot look those up in the dictionary."

"I don't, Henry."

"Yes you do!" the boys insisted.

"Tell us what are the words!" shouted one boy, and was backed up by the rest of the class in a chorus of "Yeah Yeah Yeah!"

"I don't think so, guys."

"Pleeeeaaase!" they all cried.

Henry stood up and made his case. "Teacher, it is culture, and it is history, and it is English."

Kid's gonna be a damn lawyer one day.

I sighed. "Fine."

The boys cheered.

I cleared my throat. "Charlie."

"That one is dumb," one of the boys whined. "Tell us another one!"

"Ok, let's see. 'The man in the black pajamas.'" I raised one eyebrow for effect.

---

[1] What Americans call The Vietnam War, Vietnamese call The Resistance War Against America or simply The American War.

"So dumb!" they cried. "Weak, weak, tell us the real ones!"

"What about gook, Teacher?" said one boy.

"You're a gook!" another boy shouted, pointing at his friend.

"Guys," I admonished them, "please don't call each other gook."

"Zipperhead!" the other boy exclaimed, pointing back.

The class erupted in uproarious laughter.

"If you guys already know these words, why are you asking me?"

"Because it is hilarious!" cried Henry, clutching his stomach in convulsions.

"You don't think those words are offensive?"

"Gook is our word now, and we are taking it back!" declared one boy.

"Teacher," Henry said, still laughing, "it cannot be offensive. It has no context for us."

"Context... good word, Henry," I said. "But do you think that's really true?"

"Vietnam won the war, Teacher. Are you offended if I call you a loser?"

"No Henry, I suppose not," I shrugged. "Not in that context anyway."

41
Holiday in Cambodia
ភាអាចកើតឡើងនៅទីនេះ

When I walked out of my hostel in the Cambodian capital of Phnom Penh, I was greeted by a line of tuk-tuks stretching down the street. These modified moto-cabs were parked bumber-to-bumper, the drivers all smoking cigarettes and waving at me, shouting, "Killing Fields! My friend, Killing Fields!"

Good morning to you, too...

The main tourist attraction in Phnom Penh is the site known as Choeng Ek. Located just on the outskirts of town, it is where one of the largest mass graves of people murdered during the brutal reign of the Khmer Rouge has been made into an outdoor museum.

In 1975, on the heels of the Northern victory in nextdoor Vietnam, another communist army came to power in Cambodia. They called themselves the Khmer Rouge. Immediately after seizing control, they evacuated the entire city of Phnom Penh at gunpoint.

Nearly one third of the Cambodian population — an estimated 3 million people — were killed or died as a result of the totalitarian dictatorship of Pol Pot and his Khmer Rouge. It only took four years.

Who were these Khmer Rouge? Adopted from the language of their French colonists, "Rouge" is the red color of communist revolution. "Khmer" is the native word for the people of Cambodia. "Communist Cambodia." Under order by their leader Pol Pot, the militia wore checkered red kerchiefs around their necks as they moved the urban population to the countryside.

In this "back to the rice fields" policy, there was no room for the educated. Anyone who spoke a foreign language, or who wore glasses, or who didn't have calluses on their hands, had to go.

This was the creation of a new society, where the family unit is cancelled, and where the only education is the doctrine of Angkar. Angkar — the name for the new state — was Pol Pot's twisted vision for the Cambodian people which sought to raise a conformist generation that would answer only to Angkar. This was to be "Year Zero," and it required a purge.

The greatest tragedy of it all was that the young people, the children, were tasked with the killing. Millions of souls fell under their machetes into shallow, mass graves. To this day, the bodies still rise to the surface. There is no way to identify them, as all history hitherto was scorched in order to begin Year Zero —*The State of Angkar.*

Some 40 years later, when I found myself on the streets of Phnom Penh, the tuk-tuk taxi drivers soliciting me for a trip to The Killing Fields were all middle-aged men. I think you guys are all too familiar with the Killing Fields, I thought. What better guide though, right?

I picked the friendliest looking driver and we puttered away to the outskirts of town.

The first stop was the Tuol Sleng Genocide museum — an old high school that the Khmer Rouge repurposed as a detention center for suspected "enemies of the state." Here, political prisoners were interrogated under torture. To stay alive, you learned to lie. The good liars lived. The bad liars, didn't. Lying became a virtue.

Every evening at dusk, a fresh group of those found guilty by the Khmer Rouge were marched by torchlight to Choeng Ek. To the *Killing Fields*.

The focal point of this outdoor memorial is a tall, glass tower. Encased within it are 5,000 human skulls of the victims whose heads were bludgeoned with rifle butts and whatever farming tools were laying around. Bullets were not wasted on the undesirables.

Choeng Ek is but one of the 20,000 killing sites discovered throughout Cambodia.

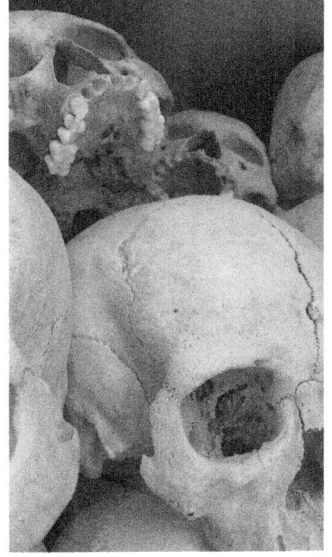

I stood there with my driver. I don't think he spoke much English — we had hardly exchanged a word all day.

"Where were you... when this was happening?"

"I was here," he said, nodding.

We stood a long time in silence.

"Did they make you do the killing?"

He stared into the afternoon sun. "We go now," he uttered finally.

This is the trauma of the Cambodian people.

But people have a way of bouncing back from even the greatest of atrocities, and the Cambodians are doing it in stride. In reclaiming their culture, they are perhaps the most positive and welcoming of any people you could hope to meet. They are also the caretakers of one of the great wonders of the world — the Ankgor Wat Temples — which are perhaps the most mystical of any monuments that I have beheld.

The story of Cambodia remains a sobering reminder that the sentiment of "It can't happen here" is the mantra of complacency — the swan song of the fool who fails to see the virus of terror at his own doorstep. The wolves are ever circling the sheep.

42

A Wet Man Never Fears the Rain
Mùa hè dài, ẩm ướt

Some places just can't catch a break. Vietnam is one of them — weather-wise.

In the south, the locals joke that Saigon has two seasons: Hot, and Wet N' Hot.

Owing to its unfortunate geographical location, central Vietnam gets three different rainy seasons per year. At least three.

But in the north, Hanoi is far and away the most temperate climate on this long coastal strip of country, with actual jacket weather in winter. Every summer, though, this capital city still gets lashed by the seasonal monsoon.

When you feel the first drop of rain, you have about ten seconds to seek shelter. It goes from droplets to deluge on a dime. Not if, but when I get stuck in a squall, I try to make the best of it. I think of Forrest Gump, and the time he spent in Vietnam. Walking down the street, I like to address other hapless, cowering pedestrians with my favorite Gump-isms.

"Sometimes it was big ol' fat rain."

Then I'll pass another poor, grimacing person. "Sometimes it was little bitty stingin' rain."

These soaked and miserable strangers will look at me quite confused. This is for my own amusement anyway. A boost for my own personal morale.

"Sometimes the rain seemed to come straight up from underneath!"

All the layers of motor oil and petrol and gunpowder that have been packed into the streets for decades come up when a gulley washer of water hits. All that gunk sloshes in the streets with nowhere to go. There's no way of avoiding it.

When I first moved to Hanoi, I packed khakis. Mistake. Every time it rained, all of that tar-black grime kicked up onto the backs of my legs. My trousers were streaked with stains that no amount of scrubbing could remove. In a single hour in August, my appearance went from sharp to shoddy.

The water on some streets will flood waist-high. People still drive their motorbikes through it, their fully submerged vehicles fanning waves of water out in either direction. I'm sure that's great for the engine.

The best way to wait it out is to duck into one of the myriad cafes in Hanoi's French Quarter. Sip a whipped egg coffee. Watch the rain dripping from the palm fronds, the puddles swirling in the street. There is a calm to this wet ambience. Safe and dry just under the metal awning of the coffeeshop.

Some of the best thoughts are thought to the sound of rain falling on tin roofs.

43

No, the *Other* Pho
Không, phở khác

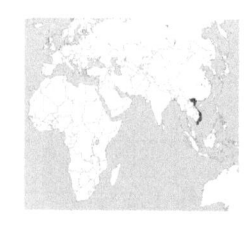

Motorcycle taxis are the primary method for getting around town in Vietnam. Just hail pretty much anyone riding solo on a motorbike, hop on, and tell them where you want to go. Always negotiate the price, of course, and if you're weird about the communal helmet, bring your own.

I had just arrived in Ho Chi Minh City (Saigon's new name as of 1975, if we want to be PC about it), and I waved down a motorbike taxi. This guy was actually legit, down to his green "GRAB" official jacket.

Grab is the motorbike Uber of Vietnam.

"Xin chào," I greeted him, hopping on the back.

"Where you go?" he asked, handing me the communal helmet. Better lice than a bodybag home, I figured, and put it on. The chin strap was missing the latch.

"Take me to the best pho," I said, pronouncing it "foe" like a fool American. "I'll buy you one."

His eyes lit up. "You like a pho?"

"I love a pho. Let's go."

I do love pho, the national dish of Vietnam. The hearty bone broth and rice noodle soup has been exported all around the world, although its popularity in America has made it about ten times more expensive than the bowl you find on the streets of Saigon.

He drove us down insane streets, ignoring traffic lights and road rules, weaving between buses, trucks, and the million other motorbikes.

We rode on and on, through avenues and alleys dotted with French colonial houses and Buddhist temples, my white knuckles gripping the back rim of the seat for dear life. How many restaurants had we already passed? The streets were lined with people on plastic stools slurping up soups. He must have a favorite place.

We pulled onto Bui Vien, the main entertainment strip in District 1. We turned into an alley off the main drag, and then another.

We were descending into the belly of a labyrinthine neighborhood. There were two middle-aged men crouching on a front stoop sharing a needle. Kids darted across the lanes, their mothers shouting at them from inside doorways. The smell of cannabis and cheap beer hung in the air, mixing with fish sauce and egg roll frying oil. It was suppertime in Saigon, wherever the hell we were, deep within this beast.

My driver stopped abruptly in front of a nondescript house with a red light glowing from an upstairs window. Ladies of the night in their miniskirts and barely legal lingerie were congregated on plastic chairs outside.

As soon as we rolled up, they jumped to, waving at me and making kissy sounds. "Sexy man, hello! What you look for, sexy man?!"

I smacked my driver on his helmet. "Hey dude," I shouted, "Where did you take me?"

He swung around. "You say you like a pho. The hook. No?"

"A hooker?!" I exclaimed. "Come on man, I don't pay for sex." I pantomimed eating from a spoon. "Pho, bro."

"Ahhh," he sighed. "You like a phở, not a phò."

"Yeah, I guess so."

I got off the bike so he could turn it around in the narrow alley. The whores came rushing up to me, grabbing and pulling on me with cries of "Hey baby" and "I love you long time." My driver revved the engine. I twisted out of their clutches and jumped back on the bike. We sped away, leaving my new, biggest fans clamoring behind us.

When we had made it out of the red light district and back onto Bui Vien, I tapped my man on the back to stop. I dismounted and handed him my helmet. "Dude. Let's just eat some soup, yeah? There's like a million places around here."

"You pay me." It wasn't a question.

"Of course, whatever. I'm just hungry, man."

He pointed across the street. "This a good phở."

"Great." I brushed myself off. "Order some of that rice wine y'all like. And something fried. I need to get the smell of hooker perfume off me."

Vietnamese, it turns out, is an impossibly tonal language. Depending on how you pronounce a word and with what inflection, you could be talking about two or even three very different things.

And the correct pronunciation of my favorite noodle soup? "Fuh-uh" with an upswing in your tone, as though you were asking a question. Unless, of course, you do want a Vietnamese prostitute.

But swing a dead cat in Saigon and you're likely to hit both.

The good stuff:
All the fixin's for phở gà (chicken phở).

44

Pipe Dreams
Thuốc lào là chết người

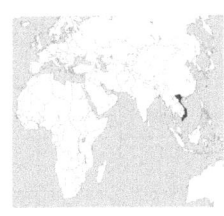

Thuốc lào is how the Vietnamese relax throughout the day. Also known as rainforest tobacco, this stuff contains about nine times more nicotine than a Marlboro. Put THAT in your pipe and smoke it.

Thuốc lào is smoked out of a điếu cày, or "farmer's pipe." It's a simple bamboo water pipe about a meter in length that is so ubiquitous on the streets of Hanoi that shops and cafes will have at least one or two leaning against the storefront.

These pipes are communal. Men pass by, grab a pipe, pop a squat, and load a bowl from their personal stash, taking a nice big hit to that music of bubbling water before they stand up again and continue on their way.

The ring-around-the-mouthpiece is a petri dish of untold bacterium that's surely responsible for every major outbreak of plague that the world has seen hitherto and into these uncertain futures...

This bong hit of tobacco straight to the head isn't just for men — old ladies are champions of the thuốc lào pipe. When you're a leathered old aunty in Vietnam, you can do whatever the hell you want, because you've seen some shit.

When I was living in Hanoi, I taught at a reform school across the Long Bien bridge.

The "Young Buffaloes" (Vietnamese slang for mischievous punks) took their tea break at the Bia Hoi across the street from the school. These fifteen-year-old kids held court on their plastic stools, passing the pipe around. All of them dressed in their mandatory school uniforms. All of them taking deep hits as though they'd been doing it for 80 years. All of them just waiting to take the piss out of me.

Sure, sometimes I'd have a cigarette in hand when I strolled up early for afternoon class. There they'd be, heckling me as I walked by. "No smoking, Teacher!" And they'd laugh and laugh.

> 40¢ a pack in Vietnam!

"No thuốc lào!" I'd yell right back, wagging my finger. Hmm. Rascals, the lot of them.

There was a time when I braved communicable disease and hit the pipe with some regularity. I didn't catch herpes, but I did catch a wicked head buzz. The last

> For a good laugh, go ahead and search youtube videos of foreigners smoking thuốc lào.
>
> Most don't fare so well.

time I indulged in the thuốc lào was in a crowded Bia Hoi parlor. A man gave me some particularly potent tobacco. I smoked it, clearing the bamboo chamber, and lost consciousness. I woke up on the ground, having fallen off my plastic stool, surrounded by a group of Vietnamese men pointing and laughing hysterically.

I decided then that my thuốc lào days were over. But, for the record, I never puked.

Tall-Tom Davies taking a pull on the thuốc lào pipe.

45

Betel Mania
သွားတိုက်ပါ

I have never been in the military, nor do I play baseball, but I still enjoy what we in the South call "dip." Smokeless tobacco, moist snuff, Copenhagen and Skoal. The stuff you shove into your gums and spit into a red solo cup at parties, guaranteeing that no woman will come within six feet of you.

I know. I'm a disgusting person.

American dip is all but impossible to find in Asia, unless you're somewhere that has an American military base.

Fortunately, there are plenty of alternatives. The tradition of chewing and spitting intoxicants is prevalent in many places. Throughout India and Southeast Asia, "betel nut" is a way of life. (Not the insect, not the Volkswagen, not John Lennon's band, but the vine that grows in this climate. *B-E-T-E-L.*)

You know you're in betel country when you see the rather off-putting smiles of locals, whose sparse black teeth appear to have been whittled into little stalactite icepicks.

You know you're in betel country when you see the blood-red spit-splatters staining the streets and sidewalks. It's an eyesore that has led to the prohibition of betel chewing in many places.

And you know you're in betel country when there's a *paan* stand on every corner. Paan is what they call this voodoo chew, wrapped in a betel leaf.

But nowhere is betel-juice more conspicuous than on the streets of Myanmar. In Myanmar's largest city of Yangon, you can't walk a block without passing a half-dozen paan stands.

You can view this disgusting photo in its full color blood-red glory at www.fermatahouse.com/itchyfeet/photos.

Each stand has a Burmese man posted up on a stool, hunched over a pop-up wooden table, rolling up carcinogenic delights for the masses. On his table you'll find a spread of fresh betel leaves and all the various fixin's for the paan:

Canisters of tobacco.

Vials of nondescript tinctures.

And always a clay mortar and pestle filled with liquified limestone — the purpose of this awful milky stuff is to cut the gums so the paan's ingredients can be absorbed more efficiently into the bloodstream.

The most important ingredient of all? The areca nut. Technically a berry, the tough, striped seed has a psychoactive effect akin to nicotine.

When in Rome... or, in my case, Yangon.

The first time I walked up to the betel man, I pointed at various and random substances splayed out on his table, like I was ordering a psychoactive Subway sandwich. He applied each ingredient to the inside of the betel leaf with surgical precision. After all, when it comes to paan, it's all about the presentation.

"Can I take a picture?" I asked out of politeness, phone in hand.

"No."

"Ok then."

"Finish?" he asked. Before I could answer, he dipped a toothpick into the mysterious vials and dabbed one, two, three tinctures onto the leaf.

"What are you putting in there now?" I asked.

"Secrets," he said with a toothless grin.

He folded the leaf three times into a wrapped wedge with one hand and held out his other hand. I slapped a tattered bill worth about ten cents onto his palm. He jammed it into his pocket and hovered the paan at my eye level.

"Open," he said, pointing the finished wrap at my mouth.

I did, and he shoved the paan right into the back of my cheek. You're not meant to bite down on the stuff. You gnaw on it. You know you've gotten to the center of the areca nut tootsie roll pop when you feel, shall we say, "lifted." That, and you spit red.

When I was a younger and puckish lad, I thought it was funny to give newbies a hearty pinch of Skoal and watch them turn green. In this Buddhist land of karma, I finally got my comeuppance.

Halfway into my first betel chew, I did what you should never do — I accidentally swallowed some betel juice. Just a little bit. I felt suddenly dizzy and the sweat spewed from my pores. My stomach flipped upside down and sent my lunch of spicy fish curry surging back up from whence it came. There was nowhere to go. I painted the sidewalk in a Jackson Pollock tapestry of greens, yellows and reds. Right there in front of God (err, Buddha) and country. Some people halted in shock. Most of them just pointed and laughed. One lady screamed and ran away.

This didn't stop me from chewing betel every single day of the 30 days I spent in that country. On day 27, I walked up to an empty betel stand beside a wheelbarrow full of salted crickets. It was unmanned, so I shouted out the greeting of "Ming-gah-lah-bah!" A boy no older than eight years old came running out from an alley and climbed onto the betel stand stool. That kid rolled up some of the best paan I've ever chewed.

Kids these days.

Every betel roll is different — from sweet to spicy, tangy to hearty. I was up to 12 betel wraps per day. Yeah, I got a little carried away. So much so that, on my last day in the country, I looked in the mirror and smiled. My teeth were stained completely red. I brushed furiously with whitening toothpaste, convinced that my mouth had gone the way of the locals.

As with most drugs, the cons outweigh the pros. In the final analysis, this subtle high isn't worth your smile.

HOW TO ENJOY BETEL
(Aka *paan*, *betel quid*, *gutka*)

1. Do. Not. Swallow.
2. Brush yo teef, son!
3. Don't say *Betel Juice* 3x in a row.

This paan from India (Varanasi paan) is regarded as the best by connoisseurs.

I Love the Smell of Silkworm in the Morning
애벌레는 분출 간다

People eat bizarre stuff all around the world, and they actually seem to enjoy it. Crickets. Spiders. Scorpions. Tofu. One of the stranger snack foods I have encountered comes out of Korea. They call it *beondegi*, and you can smell it cooking around the corner. That monkey-house, napalm smell.

Beondegi is cooked silkworm larvae.

Koreans love beondegi so much that you can buy it canned in any supermarket. I mailed my parents a can for Christmas once, along with other fun snacks such as dried squid jerky and milk-flavored soda pop. Mom forbade my dad from opening it in the house, fearing the odor would linger for weeks. Good call, Mom.

Beondegi is best "enjoyed" hot. If you follow your nose, through the streets of Seoul, you'll discover a little Korean lady stirring up a steaming cauldron of the stuff. A dixie cup's worth goes for a dollar, or 1,000 Won.

I've only ever eaten one of the little brown buggers. The hard outer shell went *squish* when I bit into it, squirting silkworm pupa juice into my mouth.

Yum.

The only way I can describe the taste is a slow burn of smoky peanut into rotten peanut into what you imagine the offspring of a silkworm tastes like.

But I still prefer it over tofu any day.

204 Letchworth

47

At the Movies
Hôn ở những bộ phim

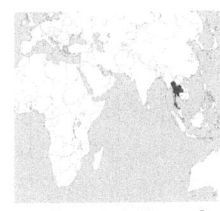

Going to the movies on a sojourn abroad can be a cultural experience unto itself. I went to see the new X-Men flick in Bangkok. Jennifer Lawrence in that blue Mystique bodysuit? Yes please.

I walked in during the trailers and found a seat. I settled in with my Big Gulp cola and jumbo popcorn. Suddenly, a very dramatic song blasted from the speakers, and everyone in the cinema rose to their feet. The person in the row behind me tapped my shoulder and whispered, "*Stand!*"

I stood with all the other moviegoers, still hugging my decadent tub of popcorn, not completely sure what was going on.

Our reason for standing was the Royal Anthem, a three-minute ceremony where everyone shows respect for the monarchy, be you Thai or not. The accompanying footage looked like a high school student's edit of the senior video collage.

Open on a panning shot of ocean waves.

Fade into a still photo of the Royal Palace.

Hard cut to high-brass military saluting the King.

Fade into school children saluting the King.

Fade into the King himself looking very kingly in his kingly red regalia.

It's a stirring little tune, sung by a woman who sounds like she's falling apart with emotion, the lyrics of which I can only imagine are something to the effect of, "Dear King of Thailand, we love you so very much, please don't throw us in jail for gossiping about your playboy ways or the fact that you don't even choose to live in Thailand."

Obviously I would never say something like that, because I love the King, and I love standing for His song, and I would very much like to keep visiting Thailand please. I promise to put my popcorn down next time.

My favorite movie theater in the world is August 8 Cinema in Hanoi. And not just because it's the cheapest ticket around at $1.50.

(75 cents on Thursdays!)

I like it because it's got character.

Imagine the dingiest, grimiest dirty-movie theater you've ever been to and use that as about a 6 on the sketchy scale. This place goes to 11.

Ok, so you've never been to a porno theater. Neither have I. But you get the idea.

August 8 Cinema has a very unassuming edifice, and you're likely to walk right past it. Its glory days long gone, it now sits in the shadow of a multiplex just one block away.

Glass doors open into an empty lobby with a desk. There is no popcorn machine, so if you have thoughts of movie-theater butter-and-salt, check those expectations at the door. They do sell "popcorn" in a cellophane bag which has been sitting on the desk for God knows how long. It's old and sticky and coated in a strange syrup that's somewhere between toffee and anchovy sauce.

The actual screening rooms are down an alley through a side door. People live here. There are dogs and kids running around, an old lady stirring a vat of phở broth over coals, and then a staircase leading up to four small auditoriums.

The seats haven't been reupholstered since the war. Those fold-out cushions contain the trapped farts from a thousand Vietnamese bottoms. They are all peppered with cigarette burns, sometimes even a massive hole between your thighs where a child who ran out of caramel fish popcorn neurotically pulled out all the cushion stuffing. It's a good thing it's dark in there, because there are some things that should never be seen in the light of day.

The last row doesn't have fold-out seating. This is the lovers' section. Two-person plush love-seats line the back wall, and yes, they are frequently occupied. Because how are you supposed to get handsy during the new *Marvel* movie with that pesky armrest in the way? These seats also have not been reupholstered or, more importantly, cleaned, since the war.

I once took a Vietnamese date to the movies and jokingly suggested we sit in the back on the make-out couches. "It is so dirty!" she squealed. We made out anyway, but like normal people, awkwardly navigating around the armrest.

The most annoying part of going to the movies in Vietnam is that the Communist Party edits R-rated films for sex and violence. I guess there's enough violence in their history and enough sex in the back row of the theater, so why overdo it?

The last movie I saw at August 8 Cinema in Hanoi was *Joker*. You know that scene where he shoots the Wall Street guys on the train?

Because I don't.

This is what I saw: Joaquin Phoenix gets on the subway in clown makeup, the drunk white collars start harassing him, he laughs maniacally, and CUT TO him running down the street in those clunky clown shoes. I think I've missed something integral to the plot here.

Even if nothing good is playing, or it's a movie in Vietnamese, it's still worth two hours of air conditioning on a hot summer's day. Hey, sit in the loveseat with a date if you want to heat things back up. Just leave your blacklight at home.

ITCHY FEET TRAVEL TALES 209

MENU

FUNCTIONAL TESTS: CHAIR (C16)

Directed by: Christopher McQuarrie

Your mission, should you choose to accept it:
Is to functionally test this chair.

Screenshot from my phone
whilst trying to buy movie tickets
in Hanoi.

48

Scamburgers in Scambodia
ហាំបឺហ្គឺណាហ្វី

Now and then, when you get tired of the local cuisine, it's okay to cheat with a western comfort meal. After endless rice and *amok* curries, my "now and then" happened in Sihanoukville, Cambodia.

Somebody recommended a local burger joint. The owner's German, he said. Wunderbar! I thought. After all, the hamburger was invented in Germany. Hamburg, Germany.

Sure enough, when I found the place and grabbed a seat on the patio, a very large German man came out to wait on me. The picture on the menu looked good. Pretty much like the burger I'd had in Hamburg's Reeperbahn district. I ordered a beer and a hamburger.

He brought the burger out and I dug right in with a big bite. It was pork. What. The. Hölle.

I called the big fella over. "Is this pork?"
"Yes."
"I ordered a hamburger. Where's the beef?"

He pointed at the menu as though I were a child. "It says ham," he growled. "So it is ein HAM-burger."

Oh no he didn't. I summoned the two semesters worth of German I took in college all those years ago. "Sie kommen aus Deutschland. Ja?"

"Ja. Sprechen sie — ?"

"Sie kennen das Hamburger komme aus Hamburg! Nicht vor 'ham.' Und sie kennen ein Hamburger ist Rindfleisch, beef, nicht Schweinfleisch! Ich esse diese 'ham sandwich' nichts! Ich nehme ein HAMBURGER."

Despite my broken *Deutsch,* I think he got the point. His face turned the color of the ketchup bottle. He told me (in English) to leave his ham sandwich restaurant, employing every English swear word he knew.

I took up my beer and obliged him. On the way out, I passed a table of Australian backpackers.

"It's pork, guys," I told them.

"Are you joking, mate?" asked the guy in the pink tank top. "It's not burgers?"

"There are no hamburgers in this land," I said solemnly.

My new best friend, the Cambodian Burger Nazi, was still shouting at me, waving a spatula. "You go! You go now! Mach schnell!"

I walked around the patio and stopped on the street. I shouted back, "Hey man, what if I was Jewish? What you're doing, with your ham sandwich bait and switch — that ain't kosher!"

I don't know how much of that he understood, and I hope this German fellow didn't just focus in on the "Jewish" part of my statement, but he came running right round that patio wielding his kitchen utensil after me. I took off, beer in hand, and ran until I reached the beach.

I leaned over the dock railing to catch my breath, checking behind me for the hulking figure of Hamburger Hitler. He was nowhere to be seen. I took a swig of my Angkor beer.

Across the street was a restaurant called "Happy Heaven Pizza." There was a giant yellow smiley face on the sign.

I smiled back.

49

Don't Worry, Be Happy
កុំប្រើគ្រឿងញៀនកុមារ

I ducked into the pizza parlor. A cute Cambodian waitress greeted me with a menu.

"You only?" she asked.

"Yeah, guess so, I —"

I was interrupted by a table of foreigners. A girl and a couple guys. The girl was waving me down. "Come join us!" she called out to me in an English accent. "The more the merrier!"

"Alright then. Cheers." I sat down.

"So where are you from?" she smiled.

"Uh, America." Whenever I introduce myself as an American, I always feel like I'm apologizing.

"What city?"

"You won't know the city. The great state of Arkansas."

"You mean, Arkan-SASS?"

"It's pronounced Arkansaw, but yeah." Blank stares. "Old French word." Still nothing. "Bill Clinton is from there."

"Hmmm," everyone nodded.

"And we've got Johnny Cash, too."

"Johnny Cash!" cried the blonde guy in the middle, and broke into song. "I hear ze train is coming. Is rolling round ze bend!"

"Yep," I laughed. "Maybe I should just lead with Johnny from now on. So, where's everybody from? I'm guessing, Britain, Germany, and…" I pointed at the other member of our party, a large and ruddy-faced fellow with a bushy beard.

"Russia!" he exclaimed, throwing his fists into the air.

"This is Yuri," said the English girl, motioning to the Russian. "I'm Caroline, and this is my boyfriend Luka."

"I'm Sam," I said. "Hello, and wie geht's, and privyet." I pulled in my chair. "Well —aren't we just World War II in a box?"

Caroline broke into Winston Churchill. "We shall fight them on the beaches and the streets," she slurred for effect, and flashed a V for Victory. "We shall defend our island!"

"We have nothing to fear but fear itself!" I chimed in with my best FDR.

"For the Motherland!" Yuri cried, beating his fist ceremoniously over his heart.

"For ze Fatherland!" Luka shouted. "I'm not doing ze salute, it looks really bad."

We all had a good laugh.

"Oh, what a shame," said our Churchill impersonator. "We were just hanging out with this Japanese guy. We would have made a whole set!"

The cute waitress came over. Caroline did the ordering. "One cheese pizza, and one with pepperoni. Sam, are you vegetarian?"

"No," I said, "hard as I try."

She finished the order with a curious addendum. "Make it extra happy, please."

"Wait," I whispered, as our waitress walked back to the kitchen. "Is this a weed restaurant?"

"Yes!" cried Yuri, and banged his fists on the table.

"Well, yeah," replied Caroline, confused. "Is that not alright?"

"Hey, when in Rome."

Cambodians have been cooking with cannabis for centuries. From restaurant to restaurant, pie to pie, slice to slice — you never know how heavy-handed the chef is going to be with the good stuff. Probably, it depends on his mood. Hence, Caroline's order of "extra happy."

This was best summated by Yuri: "Every time is different. I eat whole pizza, I feel nothing. I eat one piece, I am on a moon."

While we waited on our space pie, I engaged my new German friend.

"Hey, Luka — let me ask you something."

"Ja, ok."

"So, the hamburger is from Hamburg, Germany, right?"

"Ja, ok."

"If a German tried to give you a pork sandwich, no beef, but called it a hamburger, what would you do?"

"I vould tell zem ver zey could stick zat bullshit hamburger." He studied me with his eyes. "Zis is a strange question."

"Yes! Thank you. Danke schoen."

The pizzas came out. Thin crust cheese and pepperoni, both with a layer of what appeared to be soggy oregano.

"Is that green stuff the, uh —"

"Happy ganja!" cried Yuri, taking a slice of pepperoni and eating half of it in one bite. "Suka, blyad!" he cursed, fanning his mouth. "Is too very hot."

In the end, I had three slices. Everyone else had four, except Yuri, who had five. It was a decent pizza, but I wasn't expecting New York or Naples. I could taste the skunky flavor of cannabis with every bite.

We sat around and had some 50 cent beers, telling travel stories and sharing some laughs. Caroline and Luka had met Yuri on the nearby party island of Koh Rong, and apparently figured that he was too much fun not to keep around. I picked Yuri's brain about Russia, as I hoped that a trip on the Trans-Siberian was on my horizon.

"On the train," he said, "drink many, many vodka."

"Noted," I laughed.

Yuri leaned across the table. "For serious."

The Australians from the burger place walked in. Pink tank-top bloke recognized me.

"Hey, it's you mate!" He pulled up a chair at the next table.

"Burger dudes! More the merrier!" I went to introduce everyone. "So this is…" Suddenly I realized I couldn't remember anyone's names. "This is, uh…" I pointed at my new friends. "England, Germany, and Russia."

Caroline interjected, "Caroline, Luka, and Yuri."

"Right! And in that order!" I said. "European Theater — meet the Pacific Theater."

"Well, this must be the place," said tank-top. "Your eyes are redder than a baboon's arse, mate."

I surveyed our party. Everyone's eyeballs had transformed into glistening, cherry-ripe tomatoes. I turned back to the Aussie. "Did you guys eat those bogus burgers?"

"No way," laughed tank-top. "That guy was well pissed, yeh? He kicked us out after chasing you and closed up shop."

Cute waitress appeared at our table out of nowhere. "You pay?" she said. We all went for our money in slow motion. I opened my wallet and pulled out a wad of US and Cambodian Riel bills. Both are accepted here, but it all looked like Monopoly money to me. I picked out a $5 Lincoln and placed it on the table.

When I looked back up at my new friends, everyone had morphed into their Second World War leaders before my eyes. Caroline's face was transformed into the droopy pout of Churchill, a cigar curled in her lips. Yuri had grown a salt-n-pepper Stalin 'stache.

And Luka? Luka had sprouted a little black square of facial hair just below his nose. He eyed me sternly with cold, black eyes.

I looked down at my seat. It had become a wheelchair, a blanket draped over my lap. There was a cigarette holder between my fingers.

The pizza had gone sideways on me. "I've got the fear!" I yelled, and ran for the door.

It was early evening, but I felt much safer with my sunglasses on.

I stumbled down to the dock and instinctively joined a crowd of people. This was ok for a few minutes. Or was it hours? A man came around with a clipboard.

"Ticket?" he said to me.

"Ticket for what?"

"Ticket. For boat. You go Koh Rong Island?"

"I only had three, man. They all had more. I just ate three."

He shook his head and moved on to the next person.

I shuffled down the street. I had a beer in my hand. Had I bought another one? Was this the same bottle I'd taken as a souvenir from the Hamburgler? No, it was cold. And delicious! I could feel every bubble burst on my tongue.

A woman sauntered up to me in high heels and a miniskirt. "Hey baby," she whispered in my ear, caressing my chest. "You want have fun?"

"I think I'm already pretty happy." I looked down at her hand. It was larger than mine.

"Wait," I blurted out in my confusion, "are you a... a lady-man?"

She smacked me upside the head with that very large hand. "Lady-*BOY*," she snarled. She hissed at me and walked on with a toss of her hair.

"I'm sorry!" I shouted after her, holding my stinging face. "I'm not familiar with your pronouns. I'm on a moon right now!"

The world was an incomprehensible blur of hookers, revelers, and street food stalls. There was a boy slicing up coconuts with a machete. I realized how dry my mouth was, and I pointed at one. The boy carved it around the top, stuck a straw in it, and handed it to me.

I don't know how long I stood there, nurturing my coconut in both hands, slowly sipping the nectar. I don't know how long I was blissfully unaware of the foreign gentleman shouting in my ear. Probably for a while, because he seemed quite agitated.

"I'm sorry, I don't speak Hungarian," I managed to say.

"English, mate!" He shouted. "I'm speaking English, you knob." I picked up on his accent.

"Cheerio, gov'nah. The dog's bollocks and a leg over, innit?" I said, involuntarily mimicking his dialect.

"What's wrong with you then? I've been asking if you know where the Wat Leu Temple is."

"Listen, if you're going to yell at me, I'll have to come back later," I mumbled into my straw.

"Bloody idiot Yanks," he grumbled, and walked on.

"Hey, I'm from the South. Yankee is not the preferred nomenclature down there. Cracker, please."

This brief moment of lucidity faded back into the quicksand of my waking dream state.

Down at the beach, people were releasing paper lanterns into the sky. I watched them rise and twinkle away into the night, and I wondered where they would all come down. And where would I?

There was a dreadlocked hippie chick twirling firesticks accompanied by a tribe of shirtless drummers all dancing in a circle. I paraded right through the middle of their ceremony and continued on down the beach, seeking solitude.

The last thing I remember is watching an elaborate mating ritual of two geckos in the moonlight as they chased each other around a large rock on the beach.

Then, nothing.

* * *

I woke up to water crashing around me. I was on the beach, my toes pointed to the sea. The morning tide was coming in. My empty coconut bobbed in the surf.

Man, was I hungry. I brushed off the sand, checked my wallet and phone, and made my way back to the hostel. I passed Happy Heaven Pizza. The cute waitress was already back outside, ushering in the lunch crowd. She saw me and waved.

"You come back?" she shouted.

"No no," I yelled back. "I've had enough happiness to last a while, thank you."

"Wait," she said, and ran inside. She came out with a napkin. It was a note.

"Dear Sam," it read. "So sorry you got the fear. We are a bit too 'happy' ourselves. Take care, and catch you down the road.

Sincerely yours,
Sir Winston,
Uncle Joe,
and The Fuhrer."

ITCHY FEET TRAVEL TALES 221

> Dear Sam,
> So sorry you got the Fear.
> We are a bit too "happy" ourselves.
> Take care & catch you down the road.
> Sincerely yours,
>
> Sir Winston
> Uncle Joe
> The Führer

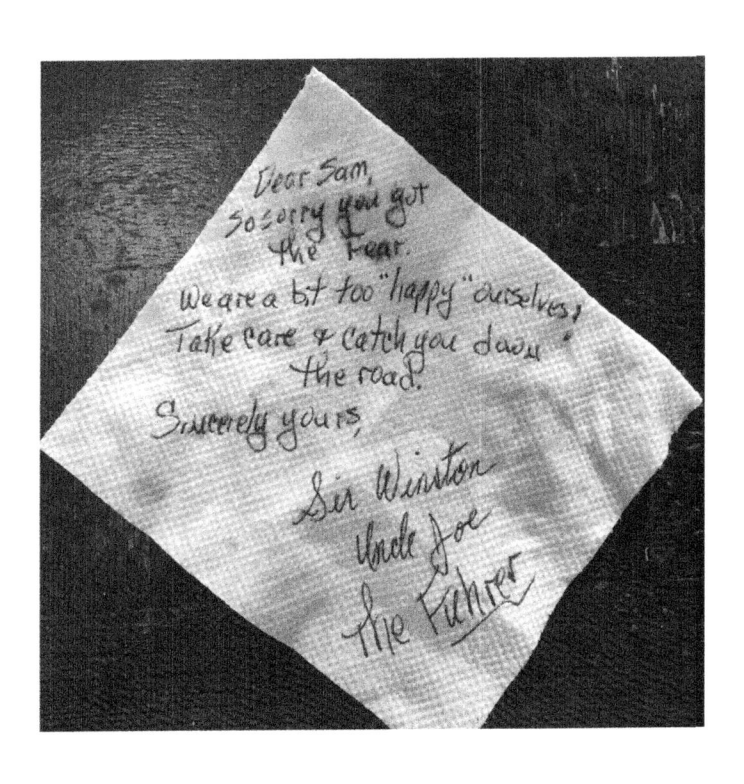

50

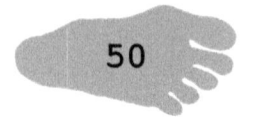

Walkabout
ဒါငါ့အဆုံးသတ်လား

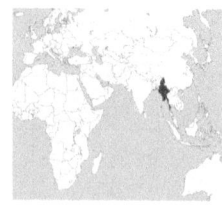

The three-day trek in the Northern Shan State of Myanmar was advertised as a "mild-effort stroll" through the countryside that can be done in tennis shoes.

This area of Shan State had only very recently been officially cleared for civilian access. By "cleared" I mean that there were still landmines out there, but the local guides, I was assured, had a general idea of where they were. It seems that Myanmar has at least three border conflicts happening at any given time, and is perpetually plagued by internal fighting.

There were six of us that showed up that bright October morning in Kalaw. There was a couple from France, a couple from Spain's Basque Country, a girl from Bavaria, our local guide Tan, and American me.

As we exchanged pleasantries and agreed (thankfully) on English, I noted that these Europeans were all sporting proper hiking boots. I looked down at my blue suede Adidas, the white stripes peeling on the sides. I was relieved when our guide Tan emerged with his Burmese longyi skirt and slip-on, soft-sole shoes.

Tan threw a satchel over his shoulder. With a warm smile he explained that we would be hiking 96 kilometers (60 miles) to Inle Lake. We would sleep in villagers' bungalows along the way. With that, we were off, ambling down water buffalo trails and into the rural Burmese countryside.

The German girl was taking a year off from academia before attending medical school, having just finished studying in Moscow. The beautiful Basque couple were on a sort of honeymoon, getting their wanderlust out before going home to make beautiful Basque babies.

Dimitri and Laura were the couple from France. Dimitri and I were the only two smokers of the group. We frequently hung back, him with his French roll-ups, me with my Burmese cheroot cigars.

Dimitri was about 8 feet tall. He had bought brand new hiking boots and was breaking them in on this trek. The pack on his back was much larger and bulkier than anyone else's.

His French accent was smooth. Not at all like the harsh, self-important Parisian dialect. His were the kind of easy, rounded tones that could narrate an audiobook.

"Laura and I are travelling Asia for three months," he told me.

"How far along are you now?" I asked him.

"Two weeks."

We meandered along ridges of rice terraces and coffee fields. As we continued climbing the hill, I couldn't help but notice an abundance of avocado trees.

Avocados the size of bowling balls littered the ground, threatening to twist an ankle out here in the middle of nowhere.

"Hey Tan," I saddled up next to our guide. "What's the deal with all the avocados out here?"

He chuckled, his eyes brightening as he kept pace with his walking stick up the winding cattle road of the Northern Shan countryside. His longyi tunic wrap billowed and flapped like a sail in the breeze. "These once were poppy fields," he said. "Many, many opium come from right here. The government say, 'No more poppy flowers,' so the farmer, he plant the avocado tree instead."

"So there's a little special magic in the soil?"

He laughed. "Tonight I will make us goku... goowahku... gawkah- "

"Guacamole?"

"Yes!"

In the late afternoon, we came upon a remote hillside village. These were the Pa'O tribe. They wore tartan-checkered turbans on their heads. On their faces, they wore smeared masks of beige thanaka paste. The women drank tea at their looms and harvested chilies, laying them out for drying on thatched tarpaulins. The men transported village goods and supplies on cattle-drawn carts.

And in every mouth was the ever-present betel nut.

The children ran around barefoot, playing soccer with a large and unidentifiable fruit.

Dimitri asked our guide Tan to call the children. At Tan's voice, they came rushing over. Tan had them all line up in a single-file queue before Dimitri, who was down on one knee and rummaging through his pack.

That's why the thing was so bulky — the French couple had brought school supplies to distribute to village children. Dimitri handed each child a notebook and a pencil. The kids all jumped up and down, squealing, and with big smiles ran over to the shade of a pagoda to inspect their presents.

This is where we would spend our first night.

We gathered around a long table beside a stilted wooden house. The women brought out Shan Htamin tomato rice cakes and a variety of fruit (many as yet unidentified). As the sun went down behind the avocado trees, I reminded Tan, "Hey — how 'bout that guacamole you promised?"

"Ah!" He smiled, then disappeared around the corner.

Chatting amongst ourselves, we had all but forgotten about it when Tan appeared with a big bowl of neon green.

That big bowl of guac went faster than my Auntie Mae's chicken salad at Bingo night.

Sorry, fellow North American country that also begins with an "M," but the best guacamole in the world is from Myanmar. Maybe it really is that "little special magic in the soil." All I know is that we slept soundly that night on the bungalow floor.

The next morning we pressed on, descending into a lush valley.

That's when the rain came.

One minute it was sunny, and in the next, the levee of the heavens broke open. It was a sudden and Biblical deluge, real Old Testament, wrath-of-God type rain. The dusty buffalo trail beneath our feet skipped the mud phase and went right into ankle-high running water.

We all moved to the grass on the side of the trail that was now a rushing runnel. Still, we were moving down the mountain slope, lower and lower in elevation, trudging along through the unrelenting monsoon.

This "mild stroll in tennis shoes" now found me crawling on my hands and knees through Burmese mud. The tread on my Adidas was worn smooth — impossible to find any traction in this muck. I was on a treadmill set on reverse. I felt like a contestant on a Japanese game show.

If I thought *my* shoe situation was rough, I had only to look in front of me at Dimitri. He had abandoned his new boots, tying them together around his neck. They had blistered his feet so badly that the blisters had opened and were bleeding.

The path wound down into a field of sodden marsh. The trail-turned-tributary of flood water flowed right into a loud and muddy river.

I've played around on plenty of rivers back home in Arkansas. I remember once canoeing in flood conditions. The rangers had closed the river. Our group, fancying ourselves old pros, put in one mile upstream where the rangers wouldn't spot us. We should have heeded their warning. That was one harrowing canoe ride, navigating six-foot swells and eddies, using the oars only for braking as we careened down the Buffalo River.

This was worse.

The sloping valley was funneling the gully washer of water straight into this channel. What was normally a stream on a sunny day was now, from the flash-flooding, a raging rapids.

Tan walked along the riverbank, his longyi hiked up above his knees, stabbing the water with a large tree branch to test its depth. The river stole it right away from him, and the branch zipped down along the current with alarming speed. It crashed into the jut of a large, sharp rock that occupied the middle of the downstream bend and snapped cleanly, its severed halves spinning into the air.

The water rose with every passing minute of rain. It was now or never, Tan shouted over the roar. We could turn around and hike the twelve miles back, or ford the rapids. He had an idea — to stack some very large rocks in the shallowest part and jam a man-sized branch into the riverbed. He would then stand, waist-deep on top of the rocks, and hold onto the tree branch. In this way, he would escort our party over one at a time.

I told Tan he was mad. "We all saw what happened to the last branch," I shouted.

He seemed supremely confident in the idea. "This is how we cross the river in Myanmar," he shouted back.

The river was 4 meters across (about 13 feet, or two Dimitri-lengths wide). We gathered the largest, flattest rocks we could find and Tan tossed them one by one into the middle of the churning, brown water. He grabbed a longer, sturdier branch from what appeared to be a downed acacia tree. Like a whale harpooner, he grasped the branch with two hands over his head and thrust it into the torrent. It stuck. He held onto it, his body splayed over the river, and plodded in to stand on top of the rock pile, forcing the branch deeper into the bed.

Dimitri went first. Tan stretched out his arm and Dimitri reached to grasp it. In he went, up to his waist. He stood there with Tan, the water rushing around them, both holding firmly to the branch. Dimitri pushed off of it, leaping safely to the other shore.

With that initial act of courage, everyone else followed suit. One by one each member of our trekking party reached out to Tan, popped down into the water, and were pulled up by Dimitri's orangutan arm on the other side.

I was last. I hovered over the bank and threw my hand out to grab Tan's. I jumped down into the fast and muddy river. My shoe slid off the rocks. The current yanked my body up from underneath me. I clung to Tan, who clung to the branch with one hand, grasping my shirt collar with the other.

I thrust out a hand to God and found it true in Dimitri's grasp.

Dimitri dug his bare and bleeding feet into the mud of the riverbank and, with two hands, pulled me up and onto the other side.

Tan was right behind me. He and Dimitri helped me to my feet. Everyone rallied around me.

"Are you ok?"

"Well," I said, forcing a smile. "I think it's safe to say my cigars are ruined."

That's not all that was ruined, of course. Now that my mortality was no longer imminent, my concern turned to my journal. It was soaked through. I had surrendered my stories to the rains of Myanmar.

A few years later, I was travelling to Europe. Paris was my port of entry, where I would have a 36-hour layover in the city.

Before I left, I looked up Laura and Dimitri to see if they were around and wanted to meet up for a drink. They weren't just around — they insisted I stay the night with them.

They picked me up at Charles de Gaule airport. They looked different out of their muddy trekking clothes — Fresh. Clean. French. We sat on the Seine and drank a bottle of wine, watching the smoke of a smoldering Notre Dame rise sorrowfully into the Parisian sunset.

When we got back to their home, there was a spread of fine cheeses and cured meats that only the French can put on.

The charcuterie was French, as was the Chateau Teyssier Bordeaux. Also French was their bulldog Marvin, who burped and snorted and farted and wheezed all over me as I snuck him little pieces of Jambon d'Auvergne under the table, his little butt ferociously wagging the little dog.

We talked and laughed over bites of camembert, poured a fresh bottle of Cabernet, and reminisced about Myanmar. The Basque couple, Laura announced excitedly, "are going to have a little one soon!"

"And what happened to your diary?" Dimitri asked.

"Oh, you don't know?" I raised my wine glass high. "Tan insisted he could save it. He sat with it over a coal fire all night and dried it out, page by page."

"To Tan!" said Laura, and raised her glass.

"To Tan," Dimitri and I chimed, and we clinked our glasses of Sauvignon a bit too vigorously. Droplets of crimson spilled out and splattered on the wood table.

"Hey Dimitri," I said. "Thanks for saving me back there. You... well, I think you saved my life."

He laughed. "I saved your life, maybe. But Tan saved your diary!"

"Are you going to publish all these stories," asked Laura, bouncing on her chair, "so we all can read them?"

"Sure," I shrugged. "Why not?" I thought for a moment over a piece of Brie De Meux. "Is it okay if I tell this one?"

"Yes!" they shouted in unison (although Laura said "oui" instead of "yes.")

"I'll change your names," I promised.

"No, don't!" said Laura.

"Of course it is okay," said Dimitri.

Marvin concurred with a wheezy, cured-ham burp.

PHOTO ACKNOWLEDGMENTS

All photos courtesy of the author except for...

Intro: Burmese Leeches and Waterlogged Words 
"Sam and Tan" photo courtesy of Laura Decamps

Chapter 1: Dropped Call 
"Squatting Toilet" by Dieter Martin from Pixabay.

Chapter 3: Some Like It Hot 
"Kimbab Heaven" photo courtesy of Danny Presutti.

Chapter 9: Trains Pains and Accidental Sightings 
"Train" by Md Faysal Ahmed from Pixabay.

Chapter 18: Grandma's Kimchi Recipe
U.S. Air Force photos by Tech. Sgt. Chad Thompson.

Chapter 18: Grandma's Kimchi Recipe 
"kim chang" by Hanul Choi from Pixabay.

ITCHY FEET TRAVEL TALES 233

Chapter 21: SPAM Donor 
"Happy Chuseok!" by Hojusaram from Flickr.

Chapter 21: SPAM Donor 
"Spam canned meat on shelves in Naha" by Dquai from Wikimedia.

Chapter 27: Spirited Away 
"Bottle 2877005" by gteddy from Pixabay.

Chapter 31: In an Octopus's Garden 
"IMG_9108" by Gaël Chardon from Flickr.

Chapter 35: Easy on the Soy Sauce, Old Man 
"Tom Letchworth" photo courtesy of Celeste Letchworth.

Chapter 36: A Whiter Shade of Pale 
Photo courtesy of Quan Vu.

Chapter 43: No, the *Other* Pho   
Photos courtesy of Quan Vu.

Chapter 44: Pipe Dreams

Photo courtesy of Tall-Tom Davies.

Chapter 45: Betel Mania

"Spit from chewing Areca nut 02" by Anna Frodesiak from Wikimedia.

Printed in Great Britain
by Amazon